PRAISE FOR *PARENTS AS MENTORS*

"An enthusiastic guide that seeks to enliven the art of mentoring for parents—and in doing so, aims to bring out the best in our children. Mentor, in the tradition of Greek mythology, embraces the finest qualities of being a trusted counselor, guardian, and teacher. This book teaches mentoring skills to parents and will be extremely valuable for anyone helping children discover, enjoy, and celebrate their natural talents. Using unconditional love as the foundation, the pages are filled with positive suggestions, narratives, and activities to try."

—Mark K. Shriver

"A 'must-read' for parents! With wisdom, warmth, and plenty of examples, here's a reader-friendly guide to raising children for the new millennium."

—Ruth H. Goldman, M.S.W., B.C.D.

"*Parents As Mentors* provides us with abundant anecdotal and research-based evidence about the development of each child's unique talents. Every parent who reads it will feel more comfortable with their role as their children's first teacher."

—Dr. Gus A. Sayer,
Superintendent of Schools, Amherst, Massachusetts

"Vitalizing and affirming of the joy and importance of parenting; an insightful, down to earth, yet sophisticated perspective on children, their development, and the opportunities parents have to nurture and share in each child's unique journey as he or she 'grows up.'"

—Charles T. Gordon III, M.D.

"At last! A book about parenting written by the real experts—two parents! Filled with great insight and humorous anecdotes, this book is a must-read for moms and dads searching for practical advice on how to rear successful kids in today's hectic world."

—Wade F. Horn, Ph.D.,
president, The National Fatherhood Initiative

Sandra Burt and Linda Perlis

Parents As Mentors

A New Perspective on Parenting That Can Change Your Child's Life

PRIMA PUBLISHING

Prima Publishing and colophon are registered trademarks of Prima Communications, Inc.

Photographs on pages 32, 77, 113, 147, 151, 157, 169, and 196 courtesy of authors. All other photographs courtesy of PhotoDisc.

Library of Congress Cataloging-in-Publication Data

Burt, Sandra.
    Parents as mentors : a new perspective on parenting that can change your child's life / Sandra Burt, Linda Perlis.
        p.   cm.
    Includes bibliographical references and index.
    ISBN 0-7615-1685-9
    1. Child rearing. 2. Achievement motivation in children. I. Perlis, Linda. II. Title.
    HQ769.B823   1998
    649'.1—dc21   98-33958
                                                                    CIP

99 00 01 02 03 04 05 HH 10 9 8 7 6 5 4 3 2 1
Printed in the United States of America

HOW TO ORDER

Single copies may be ordered from Prima Publishing, P.O. Box 1260BK, Rocklin, CA 95677; telephone (916) 632-4400. Quantity discounts are also available. On your letterhead, include information concerning the intended use of the books and the number of books you wish to purchase.

Visit us online at www.primalife.com

To the nine wonderful men in our lives:
our husbands, Barry and Jeff,
and our sons,
Aaron, Andrew, Cliff, Daniel, Jonathan, Roy, and Stephen.
Without you, this book would never have happened.

CONTENTS

ACKNOWLEDGMENTS

BEFORE WE EVEN knew each other, four people gave us the foundation for this book: our parents, Ruth and Millard Cass and Evelyn and Herbert Sacks. From their constant, unconditional love, we have reaped the rewards of a lifetime.

For this book in particular, we have been especially lucky. Our agent, Sara Camilli, like us a mother of boys, has given us her time, expertise, enthusiasm, and perhaps most important, her friendship. Along with Sara, our editor, Jamie Miller, saw the potential in our early proposal and gave us her unstinting support and assistance, even from three thousand miles away. And, seeing the "big picture," our publisher Ben Dominitz boosted our confidence with his. To Andrew Vallas, our project editor, thanks for your direction and advice; we are "resting assured." To Erin Lee, thanks for taking us step by step through the marketing process and for your caring and concern. Susan Smyth and Laura Larson, we appreciate your tremendous patience. Many thanks, also, to all the other publication, design, legal, and sales staff at Prima Publishing whose efforts have gone into *Parents As Mentors*.

The wonderful interviews we were fortunate to have would not have occurred without the kindness, wisdom, and time our "subjects" were willing to share. To Chris Wallace, Dale Anthony Stark, Ph.D., Mark Shriver, Aline Gross Sayer, Ph.D., Hon. Mary Landrieu, James Earl Jones, Diane Ippolito, Esther Heller, Ruth Cass, T. Berry Brazelton, M.D., and Debra Aaron, our warmest thanks.

Ruth H. Goldman, M.S.W., B.C.D., took the time and trouble to read an early version of our manuscript and to return it with helpful suggestions and welcome encouragement. Dr. C. T. Gordon III, M.D., Mary Griffith, Wade F.

Horn, Ph.D., Joanne Kemp, Gus A. Sayer, Ph.D., Dr. Carol Brimberg Schulman, and Lea Thompson graciously previewed sections of the manuscript and offered both their insight and support.

Special thanks to the many members of both of our extended families and numerous friends and special contacts for letting us use some of your photos and tell some of your stories. This book is yours as well.

Every day for nearly thirty years, from diapers to carpools, from the first day of nursery school through the first day of college and beyond, we have been blessed with our wonderful families. To our husbands, with whom it all began, and our seven sons (and one terrific daughter-in-law), your indelible perspectives constantly challenge, impress, and amaze us. You have patiently given us your time and advice, given up your schedules, your meals, and in some cases, even your rooms, for this project. Only you could have provided the sustenance and love we needed as we worked to produce this latest joint creation.

Finally, we recognize that neither of us could (or would) have written this without the other. We hope that our readers can reap some of the joys from this book that we have found in our friendship.

INTRODUCTION

One of the most important gifts a parent can give a child is the gift of that child's uniqueness.

—Fred Rogers and Barry Head, *Mister Rogers Talks with Parents* (Family Communications, 1983)

I N T H E M I D D L E of winter, two young women gave birth to their first children. Exhausted after hours of labor, one exulted, "Well, the hard part is over!" Her doctor, a decade older, laughed. "No," he replied. "It's just begun."

When we are honest with ourselves, parents realize we can use all the help we can get. As new mothers nearly thirty years ago, we expected that our most difficult choices would be "breast or bottle" and whether to try the newfangled paper diapers instead of the cloth ones. For any unforeseen problems, we could pick up the phone and call our mothers. Our husbands assumed, as we did, that we would be in charge of "children's issues," and they would earn the necessary living to support us.

These faded family portraits are now suitable for display with the rest of our ancestors; parenting roles and styles have undergone overwhelming changes. Dual-career families are now commonplace. There are all sorts of new family configurations. Some families have a mom but no resident dad, or a dad but no resident mom. Some have two moms or two dads. In some cases, grandparents have had to step in and do the parenting. Fathers and mothers often share child-rearing chores and decisions. Family time is at a premium in every home, and extended family, as an informal resource for on-site support and guidance, is frequently far away.

All Children Have Talent

ONE THING THAT has *not* changed is parents' desires to bring out the best in their children, whether they excel in art, athletics, or academics. In today's high-tech, education-enriched world, we and our children have many choices to investigate. At what age should a child first use a computer? What kinds of sports should we encourage a reluctant youngster to explore? When should a child begin music lessons, and how do we select an instrument? What if our youngster doesn't *have* any talents? Hold it! Here is one comforting thought: *All* children have talent. The exciting part is to find it.

How can we identify a child's talents? If he is not an artistic, musical, athletic, or academic star, what is left? Here are some samples:

- The child everyone wants as a "best friend"—the empathic listener

- The one who organizes everything she is involved in—the natural leader

- The one his peers always come to for solutions—the practical "idea person"

- The one who can get even the grumpiest kid to crack a smile and usually "breaks up" everyone else with laughter—the natural comic

- The one who even as a toddler could give accurate directions around his town—the one with spatial aptitude

- The "wheeler-dealer" who could run a profitable ice franchise in the Antarctic—the born negotiator

All of these personal skills are talents as remarkable as the familiar four we began with. All are surprisingly easy to uncover and important to encourage.

Mentoring

PARENTS AS MENTORS demonstrates how adults can discover and nurture a child's unique abilities. As parents, we are our children's first and most important mentors: their guides to life's lessons and adventures. Because this concept is what we explore, *Parents As Mentors* is both our title and our theme. Learning to mentor is part of learning to be an effective parent.

Each of the book's twelve chapters deals with a separate issue. We begin with an introduction of ourselves and our families, followed by an exploration of terms and conditions. What is talent? How can a parent best support a child's talents? Children offer clues to their strengths; we can learn to spot them. Armed with suggestions, we encourage our children to thrive. An enriched child has observant parents, an environment and resources that stimulate curiosity, and personal time and space to explore.

A child needs time alone to take charge of her own body and mind. To fill our children's time with meaningful pursuits, we might overschedule or push activities or lessons that are inappropriate. Readiness for formal study is a function of development as much as of ability. The skills most often supported by lessons are those most easily abused. Pressure to excel, brought at the wrong time, can backfire.

Crossing many skill boundaries, technology can be an asset in fostering a child's natural talent. Children have technological familiarity and comfort at increasingly earlier ages. We present guidelines to help sort out what is useful.

Parents need current information about school. We can then better evaluate how well a school meets a child's needs. We can and should develop a partnership between home and school to support a youngster's strengths. In the elementary school years, children first become involved in teams, clubs, or other groups. These are experiences to encourage; they can improve a youngster's interpersonal skills, as well as nurture her strengths.

For interactions of a different kind, home-grown talents are valuable. Family members learn from each other, and each member can support the talents of the others. Most communities have numerous resources; children can broaden their experiences and involvement in the world outside by taking advantage of these opportunities.

Getting the Most Out of This Book

SO HOW CAN you get the most out of *Parents As Mentors*? The first three chapters give a foundation for understanding what follows. Then you might want to browse; delve here and there; pursue what piques your interest or fills your need at the time. There is no prescribed order for reading the chapters. Different subjects will be useful to you at different times. The "Tips to Try" at the end of most chapters are designed as simple guideposts—helpful ideas to keep in mind.

A lot of parenting comes naturally. After all, love and caring are instinctive. They are the primary ingredients children need to thrive. As part of our research for this book, we interviewed people from a variety of backgrounds and occupations. Without exception, every one of them told us the single most important factor in the development of their self-confidence was the unconditional love of their parents. Regardless of their strengths or weaknesses, their successes or failures, children need their parents' love.

Working Together

WE RECOGNIZE THAT not every family has a parent at home each day, all day; in fact, today most homes do not. How can such busy parents marshal the time, energy, and resources to serve as mentors for their children? Stick with us; we can *all* do it! Here are some suggestions to hold onto to help you do the job. The trick is not to expect perfection; it is to expect the best in ourselves.

Time: You can't escape it. Somehow, somewhere you will need to choose time with your child over time for some other priority. You cannot go back next week to reclaim time you wish you had spent with your child. Children love to be included; if it is possible and appropriate, take your child with you: to the dry cleaners, the post office, the bookstore. More important than any gift you can buy is the gift of your time and attention. Time matters.

Talking: Conversation works two ways—talking and *listening*. In the car, at dinner, before bed, sit down with your child and let him talk with you. Even the youngest of talkers relishes being listened to. Bounce back what you are hearing; that's how a child knows you are paying attention. Every child feels valued when her parent chooses her as a conversation partner.

Mealtime: Meals don't nourish only the body. If you are not home for a family dinner time, can your child count on you to be there for breakfast? Some people make Sunday morning brunch their special family time. *When* it happens is not as important as *that* it happens.

Reading: Reading to a child enriches not only his mind but also his self-esteem. When someone who loves a child reads to him, he feels good about himself. What do you have to adapt or rearrange to find time to read? Bedtime, after supper, bath time, or any time you might switch on the TV, reach for a book instead. Whether the choice is yours or your child's, even after he is old enough to read, time together with a book is priceless.

Stress: How is it appearing in your home? Are you exhausted all the time? Is there a lot of short-tempered yelling or door slamming, or just impatience and annoyance? *Stop* for a minute! How does all this affect your child? What is *she* feeling? What might help? A short talk, a walk, music, playing a game together? Maybe having a secret signal that you share when you are too stressed to function well can alert both of you to give each other some space for a while. We know a teacher who put on a witch's hat when she was having a rough time; the class knew what she meant without any words.

Share: With another parent, a friend, a neighbor—someone who cares—share your thoughts and problems. Parenting was not meant to be done in isolation; the normal ventilation and mutual reassurance that takes place among parents is important for good mental health. Sharing your thoughts can bring an extra bonus: another family might include your child in a trip to the playground; you can then reciprocate at a time convenient for you. Carpooling is another such dividend; children usually enjoy visiting with each other on their way to lessons, errands, or appointments. Just remember, it is extremely important to children that their parent is sometimes the giver as well as the receiver.

"Stresses on parents have increased significantly. . . . Focus on the stress that's getting handed on to children. Pull back and get your values straight. Decide what you care the most about. Figure it out, and ask yourself, 'Am I really doing what I think is important?'"

—T. Berry Brazelton, M.D.,
interview with authors, January 25, 1999

Hobbies: What do *you* most like to do for yourself? What enriches you can enrich your child. If you like to paint, drape her in an old shirt and give her poster paints, a paintbrush, and a roll of shelf paper. If you work out to an exercise show or tape, your child will love doing his own version. If you are working at your computer, a young child might enjoy sitting beside you and scribbling her own messages on paper; then when you can comfortably take a break, let her use the keyboard or special age-appropriate software. Concerts in the park, art museums, or local sporting events are all exciting places for children; just remember to come prepared with stroller, snacks, and something for them to do (paper, crayons, small toys). A child's world grows wider when he goes along.

Weekends or days off: How can they work for you? Even chores can be shared. For laundry, grocery shopping, and house and yard cleanup, you can delegate responsibilities based on your child's age. Toddlers can sort clothes by color; ten-year-olds can measure detergent and turn on the washing machine. Children feel important when they are needed. What does everyone *enjoy?* Renting a movie? Tossing a football? Listening to a new CD? Let a different child choose the family's special activity each weekend. It doesn't have to last long for everyone to spend time together.

None of these suggestions is dependent on cost, material objects, or specific periods of time. Instead, each requires some juggling, some planning, and most important, making our children our priority—something *all* of us can do.

Our examples are based on true stories. As Huck Finn said, "this is mostly a true book, with some stretches." In some cases we have changed names, but personalities insist on shining through. Discovering and nurturing a child's talents is a wonderful and challenging part of parenting. Enjoy the adventure!

1

Getting to Know Us

SIX BEWILDERED CHILDREN stood in the middle of Linda's kitchen and looked uneasy, confused, and shy. Staring warily at each other, the two oldest, intense and verbal nine-year-olds, at last took off to find a board game. The next two (five and six years old) chased each other out the back door into the yard. Exploring the territory cautiously, the youngest two (eighteen months and one year old), one walking on wobbly legs and the other crawling carefully behind, headed for the toys in the corner. Because we each had three sons (of matching ages), friends had suggested we and our children would enjoy meeting.

What we thought would be a wonderful match-up of our children began inauspiciously. Since then, our boys have been in and out of each others' lives, mostly out. But the combination was perfect in an unforeseen respect—it brought the two of us together, first as parents, then as friends.

Twenty years later, these boys have grown up and been joined by yet another. They no longer stand in the middle of the kitchen floor, and in some cases, they have their *own*

1

> All children have talent, and *all* children have potential. So do all parents.

kitchens. As they continue to pursue their educations and careers in medicine, literature, engineering, visual arts, music, and classical studies, so far, what delights us is that they are happily using their abilities in productive ways. We have laughed and cried and worried over them together; we and they have made lots of mistakes. But we are pleased with the young men they are becoming. That is why we are describing what we have learned in the process. Although to us our boys are "still cooking," we are happy for them in their accomplishments so far.

Early on, we found that our parenting philosophy was the same. For us, child rearing was our most important job, to be done carefully and actively. We realized that all of our decisions about our children rested on that premise. While we recognized that we were privileged to be able to offer some material advantages to our children (in the form of lessons, supplies, or transportation), we understood that our time, attention, and concern with their interests and abilities were more significant. More important than any tangible advantages we could provide was our focus on supporting each child's uniqueness. Accepting the role of an involved participant, any parent can apply the ideas and experiences from our stories to his or her own situation. Active parenting means conscious effort; active parenting means being a mentor.

One of our big surprises as mothers was that we wound up with all sons. While we were delighted to have each one, from the very beginning we wondered about our credentials. Though we each had a younger brother, we really did not know much about boys. A friend gave us her mother-in-law's perspective: "Boys run around a lot, with sticks." That is the confused mind-set we were in as our homes began to fill up with males; we anticipated and learned to live with toy guns, mud football games, soccer balls, and slingshots.

Imagine our amazement when we discovered that in addition to all of these pastimes, boys also like sedentary activities, write poetry, love music and reading, and do all sorts of things *we* understand and enjoy. Courtesy of our "renaissance men," we have become exposed to mandolins and dulcimers, twentieth-century abstract art, frogs, newts, tarantulas, fencing, the culture and politics of ancient Rome, and some unusually fine books, movies, and music.

As we laughed over our children's antics and talked over our worries and concerns, we realized that our greatest support came from our friendship. We began to write down some of the stories we were sharing, to savor and save them. Our children were all so different from each other, and each brought us the excitement of his own individuality.

Gradually, we recognized that our philosophy was evolving. The approach we were living by was becoming a touchstone we could use as we went along. We found that following our children's interests wherever they led enriched their experiences and supported their self-confidence. They led; we followed and helped. When one showed an interest in performing, we found a community theater that needed a child for a particular show. When another wanted to run, we found a local children's track team for him to join. Neither of these children has become famous as an actor or a track star (so far!), but each enjoyed his experience and was able to apply his new skills as he grew. As parents, we supported each child's interests by finding appropriate outlets. The first part of our philosophy emerged as "actively follow your child's lead."

Tips from other parents helped us find the resources for our children's interests. Bingo! We realized that the second part of our philosophy was already in place: share problems, questions, and successes with other parents. The sounding boards other parents provide are sources of reassurance, support, and information that we all need in raising our children. Whether we are single, married, at home, or employed outside the home, parenting is a job too important to do in isolation. We need each other.

We learn from others and from experience. No one starts out knowing "how to do it." By pooling our ideas, we become resources for others—and they for us. Like life, parenting is a learning process. We are happy to share our twenty-eight years of experience, our successes and failures, but we, too, are still learning. In raising children, anyone can sometimes fall ignominiously on her face.

> Whether we are single, married, at home, or employed outside the home, parenting is a job too important to do in isolation.

Sandy: A recent train ride with three intelligent thirteen-year-olds reminded me that, as a parent, I am still growing. A former English major and erstwhile writing teacher, I was determined to provide for the boys' learning and amusement. I packed a special bag with all kinds of word games and books. Since two of the children were from the West Coast and one from the East, I thought this would be a good opportunity for them to discuss differences between the two regions. I had a complete and abrupt dose of reality when all three boys chose to spend the four-hour trip reading The Simpsons *comic books, punctuated only by assorted punches, pokes, and prods.*

Awash in layers of children, together we came to recognize that our concerns were not unique. With every age and stage came predictable issues, if not always predictable behavior. The recipes for each situation may not have been the same, but they had similar ingredients. We began to see patterns in children's needs.

Although we always aspired to be teachers, we had not realized that being a parent is also being a teacher. With each child's curious and sometimes funny encounters with his world, we had to be interpreters, sometimes arbiters, and often knowledgeable guides. But even the best of intentions can backfire.

Linda: As a dedicated English teacher, I wanted to instill an awareness of language into my firstborn toddler. Roy, two, was heading for the fountain in a local mall, squealing, "Look, Mommy, a tountain!*"*

"Roy," I gently corrected him, "that's a fountain! FOUN-TAIN, *with an "F!"*

"Okay, okay," responded the little boy. "Tountain, *with an* EPP!"

I had no need to worry or push; each child learns at his own pace. In fact, at twenty-eight, Roy says "fountain" correctly every time!

Sandy: Some of my early "teachable moments" came from my first year as an instructor in a junior high school. One of my five eighth-grade classes consisted of thirteen boys, who had all failed their grade levels at least once. My challenge, as they sauntered their way into yet another "holding pattern," was to get them to focus, to be interested, and even to learn. The goal was to make them feel they could *learn. This was my first contact with "problem" students and with behavior and learning problems as well. Lessons from these "lucky thirteen" were helpful later with my own boys.*

As their long legs and arms seemed cramped in the standard-size desks, they sat draped over windowsills and bookshelves; this was okay with me as long as they paid attention in class. It was my first lesson in one-size-(or style)-doesn't-fit-all. As I watched them struggle with their academic tasks, I also realized how much a child's self-esteem is connected with how the adults in his daily interactions view him. The assistant principal, a cartoon of a little man, brisk, self-important, and concerned primarily with infractions of rules, paid frequent visits to my class when the lucky thirteen section was present. He assumed that for every misdeed in the school, he would find the culprit among them. While the boys were angry and insulted by his constant insinuations, after years of such treat-

ment, they also expected it. I recognized how important it is for children to receive respect to feel worthwhile. Like adults, only when children feel important themselves can they care about the others around them. These boys had never been considered worthy of respectful treatment; it was not surprising that they did not value most of the adults they encountered.

One day I, too, did not level with them and found out quickly what an error this was. It was winter, and a sudden New England ice storm had coated all the trees, wires, and roads overnight. In the morning, the hardy ventured out, but, having grown up further south, I was not about to leave the safety of home. I called school and reported that because of "car trouble" I would be a bit late. Later that day, after the ice melted and I arrived, my thirteen boys found me between classes. "Mrs. Burt," they chorused, "can we take a look at your car? We're really good at fixing things; maybe we could help." I should have explained that the trouble with the car was that there was a chicken behind the wheel. I did learn that under the toughest exterior is sometimes the kindest heart. No one in any of my other classes had asked why I was late or what had befallen me that day.

From our teaching experiences, we learned how different children can be and how much they value our recognition of them. For a period in our lives, each of us was fortunate enough to be a full-time parent. During this time, we used our interests to volunteer in parenting and community organizations; eventually, we even founded and ran several. These were important times for us. Our adult activities enriched our lives and those of our families. The knowledge we gained and the people we met broadened our awareness of what children need and what we could do to support them.

Linda: *We each went back to school for a while, Sandy to resume teaching (this time at the college level) and then to pursue graduate work in child development, and I to study television production. Sandy became an educational consultant in private practice, and I became a television and video producer. Meanwhile, we continued the parenting demands of scheduling,* *carpooling, and volunteering.*

As our boys grew, other people began to ask our advice, so we organized HUG—Helping Understanding Grow. Through HUG, we spoke, as experienced parents, to local community, school, and parenting groups about various child-rearing issues. What surprised us most was the hunger parents expressed for communication with and support from other parents. Groups of parents were replacing what used to be nearby extended family or small, close-knit communities.

Expanding on this trend, we developed "Parents' Perspective," a public service radio program devoted to parenting issues. Each week, we interview guest experts on topics such as communicating with your child's school, helping children resist bias, and the benefits of peer mediation. Even though our own boys are now young men, our excitement for learning about families and children continues. In a significant way, all parenting consists of on-the-job training.

> In a significant way, all parenting consists of on-the-job training.

Sandy: All parents begin with their own strengths. As a day-dreaming nine-year-old artist, I spent all my free time drawing fashion models; Linda, as a savvy eleven-year-old, frequently finagled desirable items from her next-door cousin by convincing her it was "National Trading Day." We grew up to become "patrons of the arts" in our own homes and negotiators by necessity.

Linda: Sandy, the little girl who spent hours rearranging tiny furniture in her dollhouse, never expected her adult home to be richly decorated with science experiments and assorted musical instruments and electronic equipment. An enthusiastic seamstress, I welcomed my high school graduation gift of a sewing machine, but I grew up to use it for attaching name tags to my children's camp clothing and patching worn knee holes in countless pairs of jeans. Things change.

Sandy: I always liked to sing. Twice a year, until I went away to college, my family took the six-hour drive to visit my relatives in Virginia Beach, Virginia. Along the way, my brother, sister, and I played a variety of song games and engaged in numerous arguments about the tunes or lyrics. The family often sang together, enjoying popular songs or old favorites. No longer.

As the mother of musical sons, my input is nil. No one cares to sing, but all four have had specific, and often changing, esoteric musical interests over the years. On our car trips, I have learned about the rock groups of the past twenty years from one son; about minimalist compositions and Irish folk music from another; about Baroque, Romantic, and twentieth-century composers from a third; and about classical guitar works from the fourth. As a mother, my job is dividing the family's listening time between CDs of competing and diametrically different genres and trying to induce the other three sons to appreciate the choices that were not theirs. Sometimes on the rare occasions when I am in my car alone, I close all the windows and just sing.

Linda: *One of my favorite places as a child was the finished basement my father and uncle had built. Here I had my chalkboard, my dollhouse, and lots of space to play in. My little brother, next-door cousins, and neighborhood friends also came to play here. I was the teacher; I convinced them to sit down in front of my chalkboard and taught them whatever I felt was important for that day. When I had read a Clara Barton book, I taught my "class" about nursing. When I had read about the Bobbsey Twins, my "class" wrote stories. I learned early to use snack time as motivation for my "students" to pay attention, understanding that, like an army, a class travels on its belly. I also discovered that I was capable of organizing*

"Self-image is the most important thing a parent can give to a child. Every time a baby looks at you, smiles, and you smile back, you are giving back a sense of importance."

—T. Berry Brazelton, M.D.,
interview with authors, January 25, 1999.

and managing a group; little did I realize that in motherhood I would some day find much use for those skills.

One of the most significant parts of our growing up is that we each got married and have stayed married for over thirty years. Although we realize that this scenario is not the same for all parents, we are grateful for our families' stability. Still, we have found that talented parents come in singles or pairs. The number of significant adults a child has is less important than the kind of parenting they provide. Because we have not raised our children by ourselves, our husbands deserve a brief introduction. As each of our sons and all of our relatives and friends will attest, our husbands' input mirrors their unique styles.

Sandy: *My husband Jeff is an adoring father who, if he had had his way, would have had a dozen children. An international lawyer, he has not let his frequent overseas commutes prevent him from sharing important events in our children's lives. And the boys know the best times to get in touch with their dad: when they need advice, when they need support, and, of course, when they need money. For a period after each new son was born, Jeff generously took over the grocery shopping. The older children knew enough to go with him. When they arrived at the store, Jeff always looked at his list, sized up the crowd, and declared, "Each of you guys, take your own shopping cart, and I'll meet you in twenty minutes at the checkout counter!" It is a wonder the store's manager did not roll out a red carpet when our car pulled up.*

Linda: *My husband Barry never has any trouble being recognized; his bright, colorful clothing selections are familiar eye-catchers. A business executive and head of charitable organizations, he has many passions. Beekeeping, metal sculpting, photography, and antique armor are just a few of his interests. Although he usually concerns himself with sites and designs for business expansion, his favorite construction project was the clubhouse he, our children, and their neighborhood pals built in the backyard. Despite all of his varied interests, Barry's favorite conversations are talks with his sons.*

Just like their fathers, all seven sons have their own special personalities. Aided and abetted by a beautiful coterie of nieces, nephews, and children of friends, our inspiration remains our own growing boys. We could never have fabricated their special slants on life, their unusual creations, and their hilarious responses. Although most are long past youthful words and deeds, the people they were remain the people they have become.

Linda: Right from the beginning, it was clear that my three boys were all going to be very different from each other. Roy, now a married man, has always been intense and very curious about the world around him. Question followed question while he was growing up, and, driven to high standards for himself and others, he demanded immediate answers. A talented writer and an avid reader, he would read whatever books were piled up next to his bed and then announce, "Mom, I'm out of books!" and it would be time for another trip to the library. Beginning with his interest in computers at age nine, Roy became fascinated with artificial intelligence and then with the human brain. A self-starter, he was determined to attend a university where he was free to design his own program (in neuroscience and religious studies). After obtaining his M.D., he began a residency in psychiatry. He is under strict orders not to analyze too closely the behaviors of any family members!

Tall and personable, Cliff has always demonstrated the strong negotiating skills of a true "middle child." Adventurous and enthusiastic, he is willing to try anything new and interesting. He always reaches for the hardest goals, and he both wins and loses graciously. Like his father, he is happiest when involved in many different activities. Beginning in the fourth grade, when his teacher assigned him the part of Martin Luther King, Jr. in his jail cell, Cliff has demonstrated consistent dramatic talent. He was equally comfortable with adults in community theater productions and with his peers in school shows. His empathy for others was particularly evident when he was a peer counselor in college and remains a trademark as he pursues his studies in medicine and bioethics.

Always enjoying physical activity, he and his old friends from high school still gather to play the neighborhood "turkey bowl" football game on Thanksgiving morning.

Like his dad, Aaron loves to be different; he borrows his father's colorful ties and shirts and goes through frequent changes of hair style. A sensitive and caring young man with many interests, he loves animals and is currently raising a rabbit, a dog, a flame-bellied toad, and a tarantula. His volunteer work with a local veterinarian became a paying part-time job, followed by more volunteer work at a wildlife sanctuary, and consideration of studies in veterinary medicine. From his days as a middle schooler, he has especially enjoyed musical performance and, with his comic flair, is a valued member of his college singing groups. A classical studies major, he also has a natural bent for business; during a summer job with a local real estate investment trust, he jokingly told me I could reach him at the office—"Just call and ask for 'the mogul.'" One can only hope!

Sandy: *My variety of males all began, interestingly enough, with three versions of the same face, which makes identifying their baby pictures a challenging indoor sport. The fourth, a real soul-mate of his father, looks just like him.*

When Stephen, the oldest, was born, Jeff hurried back from the hospital nursery. "You're not going to believe this!" he panted breathlessly. "All the other babies are fast asleep, but Stephen is wide awake and looking around!" It was a telling start. Fascinated with the world, Stephen has always been intense and curious, with a spongelike ability to remember whatever he encounters. From the time, at nine, he found an old chemistry textbook in the basement and read it cover to cover, he has always loved new ideas. His artistic flair and interest in writing were combined in his unusual comic book creations beginning at seven. His love of music was obvious by eight, when a week before his first piano lesson, I found him at the keyboard, studying a music book. "Mom," he explained, "I can't just start piano lessons without knowing anything!" Attempting to choose among his myriad interests while in college, Stephen decided to become a poet and literary critic, where his subjects are unlimited. Now a Ph.D. candidate, he especially enjoys bringing out the literary talents of his students. But however scholarly his letters, he still addresses his envelopes to my parents "Grandma and Grandpa."

"Coloring outside the lines" was a phrase designed for Daniel. A creative free spirit, Dan has always seen possibilities that others overlooked. Expressed most often through music and art, his talent often gives his viewers and listeners different and unusual perspectives. He added composing music to playing violin, piano, and electric guitar in high school, taking custody of our family's piano as soon as Stephen left for college. Leave it to Daniel to be a member of several bands simultaneously. When he graduated from college (an institution with a well-known music conservatory), an underclassman complained, "Now I don't know what we are going to do about music around here!" His sensitivity to people appears in his creative writing, photography, and videography. When he is not on tour with his band, he continues to grow, through coursework and employment, in his other artistic fields. Daniel is also the movie critic his youngest brother can count on to supply films his parents would never select.

With his quiet passions for both the creative and the technical, Jonathan has always managed an interesting balancing act. After Daniel left for college, Jonathan quietly took his place at the piano and began to compose. His music reflects his gentle, intense, almost spiritual commitment to his world. His love of living things surfaces in his insistence on "humane" hooks when fishing (he always returns the fish to their environment) and his refusal to eat any endangered or non-farm-raised species. Consumed with the mechanics of movement and flight, Jonathan reasons in mathematical and mechanical terms. He can spend hours perfecting his original designs. His dilemma as an undergraduate student is how to take all of the music and engineering courses available—before tuition funds run out.

For his first words, I am sure Andrew was trying to say, "Can we sue?" A born negotiator, he has always looked at the components of a situation from many angles and is quick to formulate

solutions. With an avid focus on people and international af-
fairs, even at thirteen, Andrew loves to travel. With high goals
and strong self-direction, he embraces every interest keenly.
"Mom," he announced at age four, "I need to learn to read this
afternoon, *and I have brought along some books you can use to*
teach me." As the fourth musician in the family, he consciously
sought an instrument and a perspective of his own, and he settled
happily on classical guitar. With three older brothers, he is quite
comfortable in the company of giants, especially if there is any
negotiating to be done.

All very different
from each other, our
seven young men are
motivated from within.
Pursuing their own di-
rections, they have often
led themselves—and
us—into new and excit-
ing areas to explore. As
our sons have grown,
they have tried to edu-
cate us from their early college treatises to publications in
their grown-up careers, in poetry, medicine, and literary criticism. We have read them all and understood some. We look
forward to seeing the films of one, the writings on medical
ethics of another, the contract negotiations of a third, and
perhaps the legal briefs of the last. Whether or not we can
catch the nuances or even the drift of these works of art and
science, we hope our boys catch the idea that what they do
will always be valuable to us. After all, they have given us our
most important careers. Some of the stories we tell are theirs,
but many are about other children. For the sake of privacy,
we have sometimes changed the names in the stories.

Although these seven have found their own ways to excel, what we have learned as parents is that *all* children have
talent, and *all* children have potential. So do all parents. The

> What we as parents can expect is to grow, to learn from our mistakes, and to have respect for our own efforts.

challenge is to identify and support what is appropriate for each child. Whether a child spends hours playing basketball on the neighborhood lot or goes to basketball camp every summer, whether she plays clarinet in the school band or studies music privately, with encouragement every youngster can thrive.

Good parenting does not depend on money. No matter what the circumstances of his life, a child needs adults who care. A parent knows his own child best. Parenting is not magic; we cannot expect to do it all. What we can expect is to grow, to learn from our mistakes, and to have respect for our own efforts.

A PHILOSOPHY TO BEGIN WITH

1. All children have talent and potential.
2. So do all parents.
3. Raising a child is a parent's most important job.
4. Active parenting requires conscious effort.
5. Follow the lead of a child's interests.
6. Share problems, questions, successes, and failures with other parents.
7. Remember, parenting involves learning.
8. We can learn from our mistakes; we can respect our efforts.

2

Coming to Terms

BATTERIES AND WIRE trailing behind him, Jordan ran through the kitchen one winter afternoon. Clearly, he was working on a complicated contraption, the result of a lot of planning. When asked about it, the five-year-old inventor responded with enthusiasm, "Oh, Mommy, where can I plug this in? It's going to be so great! I'm making an electric flashlight!"

Whether they are making electric flashlights or organizing neighborhood carnivals, children have talents that are uniquely theirs. Jordan, puttering in his own basket of leftover wires, batteries, and parts of broken household items, had the freedom to use his creativity. When we recognize children's strengths, we help them function at their best. The resulting self-confidence spills over into everything they do: at school, with their peers, in their choices of careers and mates.

As nurturing adults, we have the opportunity and the obligation to discover and support our children's abilities. Children deserve adults who:

1. Appreciate individuality

2. Respect choices

3. Encourage interests

4. Stimulate new interests

5. Support activities

6. Allow changes

7. Accept a unique pace

8. Provide responsible guidance and supervision

When we supply these supports for our children, we offer them gifts to grow on. Remember that as parents we are their first and most valued mentors.

What Is Talent?

TALENT IS WHAT we are good at. Lena, a little girl who brought together the neighborhood children for games and dramatic productions, grew up to be the mommy who drove two carpools in nearly opposite directions at once, with the fam-

ily dog in her lap. Lena demonstrated a talent for organization. Children can be talented leaders, gardeners, and mechanics; they can be musicians, poets, and mathematicians. Talent is the strength that comes from each person's unique way of operating in the world.

When parents nurture children's creativity, we nurture their talents. Creativity is original thinking. When children are creative, they see problems differently. They produce something new to them. They are comfortable working outside

what for them, at least, are traditional boundaries of thinking, acting, or producing. When small children line up boxes
or crates they can sit in and play train, they are being creative. When they discover that tapping on a glass of water
produces a sound, and then arrange glasses with different levels
for a variety of sounds, they are being creative. Flexible parents understand that the freedom to create does not require
mastery of a particular process. Children can create music,
sculpture, and number games without ever becoming musicians, sculptors, or mathematicians.

Knowing they have special capabilities empowers children. It gives them a feeling of importance. They receive
stimulation, self-satisfaction, recognition, or status when their
abilities are acknowledged. In one elementary school, each
child's birthday is recognized with a birthday badge. When
the child receives her badge in a ceremony, the teacher recites
her "best" qualities from a list her classmates have made and
written on her badge. "Darlene is funny, good at puzzles, a
great story writer, has pretty hair, is a super outfielder. . . ."
For her special day, each child is an important person. When
a child accepts what he can do, it will be easier for him to
acknowledge (later) what he cannot.[1]

1. Appreciate Individuality

*Sandy: As the boys worked on myriad projects, my house was
usually awash in clutter. Daniel's room was a study in contrasts—
clothes on the floor, books and papers in haphazard array on
every surface, along with a large potted palm he lugged home
from the supermarket and a metal owl sculpture he found in an
alley. One day, an old ski appeared, which was soon joined by
coils of wire, nails, nuts, and bolts all over his rug. It was only
when Dan needed to transport his latest work to school that he
explained the object was his independent project for physics: an
electric guitar he made from a ski. An exceptionally creative child,*

Daniel was lucky enough to have his own space, his room, where he could pursue his ideas with few limitations.

Children are all different. The father who buys a football for his newborn son reveals certain expectations that might or might not be realized; he might hope his son will be the athlete he never was. Given room to express himself, a child can delight his parents and himself with his uniqueness. Often abilities do run in families, but a parent's talent might differ from his child's. We do ourselves and our child a favor when we show her that we value her abilities at least as much as our own, even if they straddle two different areas. Musical parents need to be proud of their budding gymnast, and the gymnast needs to be comfortable with his athletic skills. He can appreciate music without having to create it.

2. Respect Choices

IN A MAJOR departure from the norm, one mother spent her child's toddlerhood following garbage trucks, because her son loved to watch them work. While other toddlers and parents spent time at the playground, this mother followed the grunts of garbage trucks from one subdivision to the next with her delighted two-year-old plastered to the car window. As he grew, this child developed interests in music and sports. Happily for his mother, those activities did not require driving around behind garbage trucks; she only had to go to recitals and games. In his home, this youngster's developing interests were encouraged. When last heard from, he was a self-assured, sociable adolescent, with no discernible interest in garbage (especially in taking it out).

> Children thrive when they do what they enjoy.

Children thrive when we encourage them to do what they enjoy, as long as it engages their creative or cognitive abilities or talents. At eleven, Derek had a lot of energy and

"Give children the latitude to make their own choices."

—The Honorable Mary Landrieu,
U.S. senator (D-Louisiana), interview with authors, July 9, 1998

two brothers who liked solitary, sedentary play. He was especially interested in his personal space, rearranging his bedroom on a weekly basis. As the family's self-designated architect/space planner, he took on as his first (and extremely unwilling) client his younger brother Jason. Their project was a renovation of Jason's closet, reorganizing his toys, clothes, and collections. This was a prodigious feat, falling short of artistic expectations only when they were forbidden to remove the door. The project did net Derek a playmate/accomplice and an outlet for some of his talents.

We might not all be comfortable with a youngster's total rearrangement of his room, but we can give him some latitude in areas that are natural for us, like his own bookshelf or nightstand or a wall with a large cork display board for his treasures. Children enjoy found materials like fruit crates or egg cartons for collections or keepsakes. Flexible parents try to respect a child's perspective. Like all of us, he needs some space to call his own. Within whatever limits we are comfortable setting, we can let him have some freedom.

What children are exposed to can profoundly influence their interests. Alert and aware more than parents realize, children soak up the atmosphere around them. The music a young child hears, for example, becomes what he is initially most comfortable with, because it is familiar. Three-year-old Bonnie has always been surrounded by classical music. When she was a baby, a radio in her bedroom softly played the local classical station; her father enjoys his favorites from his own collection. When Beethoven's Fifth Symphony is played, no one can bother Bonnie; she sits quietly, concentrating.

Linda: With many opportunities to enjoy animals, Aaron learned to appreciate them. At home, it is normal to have reptiles and amphibians, a tarantula in a cage, a backyard frog-and-fish pond, as well as a rabbit and a dog. When he was younger, Aaron and his dad explored natural surroundings, filling the house with books and photographs of insects and animals. As a teenager, Aaron found a summer job with a veterinarian and enjoyed his work so much that he continued it part-time during the school year. Children thrive when they do what they enjoy.

"My grandmother told me I was so good with babies!"[2] Starting when he was around five or six, this young boy took care of all eight or nine of his younger cousins at family gatherings. Interested in "what made them tick," he learned what kept them happy and safe. For his aunts and uncles, he was always the natural choice to watch over their little ones. He grew up to be the choice of many other young parents; his name is Dr. T. Berry Brazelton.

So what should parents do? *We can be receptive to our children's enthusiasms, whether we have one hour or ten.* Many activities do not require an adult on-site for long periods of time, but all activities require some encouragement. The child who wants a crab net to play in the creek needs to have or make one. The child who wants to learn about vintage planes needs to read about them or even go to see some, if he can. Every home can have some music, whether it is from a radio or an instrument; some reading material—magazines, books, or newspapers; some accessible artwork, from postcards, souvenirs, or photographs to posters or family creations. Weekend or holiday outings to museums, nature centers, historic sites, performances, and parks inexpensively give a child new insight into the world around him. Even if we have little time, we can schedule a special activity to anticipate and enjoy. A stimulating environment is where interests grow.

3. Encourage Interests

WHEN A CHILD shows a specific interest, he needs his parents' help, if at all possible, for transportation to activity sites, supplies, equipment, or even finding people to serve as teachers or mentors. Fourteen-year-old Marty juggled. His mom located a juggling club where he and his father went on Friday evenings. In elementary school, Donald was fascinated by computers. His parents found a program with a mentor who worked with him once a week. Mentors can be volunteers; they do not need to be high-priced tutors. An interested neighbor, a store owner from around the corner, or a member of Big Brothers, 4-H, or the Boy Scouts can be a mentor. A mentor might have an interest in common with the youngster but primarily must see the child as special. Mentors become involved.

Parents, as mentors, have a *special* role. Their encouragement can foster the growth of a skill or interest that might otherwise have languished. Plants, animals, and people all need stimulation to grow. The ways we provide stimulation can be as varied as our own personalities and interests. Leroy loved erector sets. He liked to figure out how things worked, especially things with batteries and wires. His dad, an avid ham radio operator, let him learn how to use his equipment, so Leroy's interest developed into a skill. In addition, his time with his dad created a special bond.

> Plants, animals, and people all need stimulation to grow.

When parents add themselves, they add a distinctive ingredient to an activity. Like Marty's father with his juggling, a parent need not be an expert to participate. Whatever time we can offer and however available we can be are as important as anything else we provide. *Children appreciate the gift of ourselves more than any tangible possessions we can offer.*

4. Stimulate New Interests

WHEN A CHILD enters a new school, a new school year, or begins a new camp experience, he is likely to be exposed to new options. There may be macramé, rock climbing, or foreign language immersion offered in a new environment. Parents can encourage a child to explore what is unfamiliar. Delving into unfamiliar areas is the way children learn: to walk, to talk, to climb a tree, to use the telephone. New interests also lead to new friends, and new friends lead to new interests. Asher's new friend Gordon had a pet iguana. Gordon's house was full of animals. He showed Asher how to care for lizards and loaned him books on reptiles. Armed with new knowledge and encouraged to do what he enjoyed, Asher became the proud owner of his own pet lizard. He learned to care for something dependent on him and to be responsible for planning and carrying out chores such as buying its food, keeping the water dish filled, and maintaining a healthy environment. He does not have the luxury of forgetting to respond to the needs of a living being if he wants his pet to survive.

Parents need to be flexible. One father cringed whenever he came in contact with a dog; now that his family has a dog,

"My family never once said I shouldn't do this or shouldn't do that. We were always encouraged to try everything."

—D. Anthony Stark,
composer, interview with authors, June 29, 1998

he has learned to relax with a pet sitting at his feet. By our example, we encourage flexibility in our children. Sometimes children see themselves as able in only one category, such as an athlete in a particular sport. Adults can show how different facets of the same discipline can be related. The Ripken boys (of baseball fame) grew up playing soccer and basketball, in addition to what became their "chosen sport." Their parents encouraged them in a variety of physical activities, enabling them to develop their athletic skills in several areas, some of which were to be helpful in their careers. Only later did they focus more specifically on baseball.

5. Support Activities

"RESEARCH SHOWS THAT the determinant factor in whether or not [a] young person's talent blooms is the support [and] encouragement . . . offered by parents."[3] Unlike Douglas MacArthur's mother, who moved to West Point when her son became a cadet, most parents can encourage their children without extremes of cost or effort. *First and most important is listening.* When nine-year-old Shira asked to try horseback riding, her mom, who knew little about the subject, had to do some research. She found a local stable where Shira could learn about horses. She enrolled her in Saturday morning horseback riding lessons and, through the instructor, found another family to carpool with, providing the support her daughter needed. Shira's interests spread to other animals and to studying animal behavior and biology. She is now in veterinary school.

A parent's lack of experience with a child's new interest does not preclude providing help. A budding high school crew team was formed by the rowers' parents, most of whom had little or no experience on the water but a lot of enthusiasm for their children's new activity. They did have experience in raising funds, which was the talent the crew team needed most.

A child who wants to play a musical instrument deserves the chance to try. Besides being an important emotional and creative outlet, music teaches self-discipline through the necessity of practice. Instruments can be borrowed, or rented at low cost, through some schools and music supply stores, or purchased used through second-hand stores, classified ads, or music school sales. Even if she does not turn out to be a concert bassoonist, a young person can experience an appreciation of how to create music on her instrument of choice.

Our respect for our children gives them the confidence they need to move in new directions. When children know that we value their interests and efforts, they feel capable. Faced with fresh opportunities, they will be more likely to attempt new challenges.

Sherman, who was often uncomfortable with physical sports, wanted to play gym hockey when he was in fifth grade. His parents found a neighborhood league, and he enthusiastically participated. Though he was one of the team's least skilled members, he loved to play. There are rewards for children when they try something new: skills gained, friends made, or just recognition for trying. In a pep talk to his gym hockey team, the coach said, "I want you *all* to play like Sherman. He gives 110 percent every time." Sherman beamed.

6. Allow Changes

AS ADULTS, WE change our minds about a lot of things; we may rearrange our furniture or the pictures on our walls. We may sign up for an aerobics class and, at its completion, switch to yoga. Our children need to have the same freedom. They should know it is okay to stop one activity and pursue something else.

Jake, a quiet, careful model airplane builder, decided that he wanted to take karate. He drew pictures of karate positions and practiced what he thought were karate moves. At age nine, he took his first karate class. It was in a large gymnasium, with lots of noisy children and observing parents. The shouts of the instructors echoed off the tile walls. He stood in a line of ten children with ten behind him and ten more behind them. They all had to kick and lunge in unison, yelling the karate calls each time. Amid flailing limbs and the echoing din, Jake looked as though he were a small calf caught in a stampede. After a few weeks, he decided he was not so ex-cited about karate any more and wanted to spend his spare time on his model airplanes. His mother agreed.

Sometimes children change their minds for the wrong reasons. When swim team practice interfered with Girl Scouts, Eleanor wanted to quit the team. Her mother helped her devise a schedule where she practiced two out of three sessions, leaving the third day free for scouting. Adult judgment can help a child determine whether or when it is time to make a change. Alden, happy with his guitar playing and feeling very sophisticated at age ten, insisted he was ready to try an electric bass guitar. He lobbied his parents to help him buy one and talked about its purchase endlessly. His guitar teacher had a different idea. "Wait a little longer," he advised, "and I'll help you learn it when you're ready." Realizing he was not quite ready, Alden agreed to wait.

7. Accept a Unique Pace

MANY PARENTS HAVE seen the "piano syndrome"—children who have shown an early interest in music, are eagerly signed up for lessons at four, only to lose interest by eight. Although prodigies do exist, we need to know what is age-appropriate skill development for our children's activities. Many schools begin music exposure, for example, with rhythm instruments and later introduce students to the xylophone or recorder. Only when children are old enough to take responsibility for regular practice (usually between eight and ten) are they ready for training in such areas as music, drama, and many sports. Even the prodigy Leonard Bernstein was not limited by having to wait for lessons until he was ten. The physical development of the brain does not permit very young children to develop specific skill training. Reading music requires the coordination of vision, hearing, and motor patterns beyond the brain development of most preschoolers, even talented ones. A child's "inner clock" is the most accurate timepiece we have.

Children vary in their approaches to an interest or skill. Where some children would enjoy just being taken sailing, Mason was determined to learn seamanship and navigation. Dragging his father along, he enrolled in boating courses and became a certified seaman/navigator. Dad knew the boat's owner, so he still got to pilot once in a while. Children have a natural sense of their own pace. They realize when they are ready to kick a ball with their friends or to join a soccer team.

> A child's "inner clock" is the most accurate timepiece we have.

Dotty, who preferred to invent her own games, left her soccer team by the time she turned nine, because she did not like the constraint of rules and practices. On reaching the same age, her sister Anita had become a natural athlete and craved structured competition. Both girls knew their own preferences; their parents knew enough to honor them.

When well-meaning adults attempt to manage a child's choices, he might abandon his new activity altogether. When Sarah showed an interest in stamp collecting, her uncle presented her with his cherished collection. Overwhelmed by the stack of filled albums, Sarah chose to proceed stamp by stamp with her own discoveries. In this way, she was in charge of building her collection to suit herself. Her uncle's albums sat quietly on a shelf.

> "**B**e aware that a child does not develop according to a clock. Each child develops at his own pace and within his own pattern."
>
> —Esther B. Heller,
> guidance counselor, interview with authors, July 9, 1998

It is characteristic of children at several developmental stages to have intense interests for short periods of time and then move on. Supportive, rather than directive, involvement works best. When we allow our children to be in charge of their hobbies, rather than prescribing their choices for them, we enable them to enjoy what *they* like. They can direct their activities in a way that is most comfortable for them.

Our homes may become repositories of collections. Their accumulation can recall a history of each child's interests. Dean always loved to collect. First he hoarded buttons, then beads, then moved gradually on to weightier objects: rocks. Depending on the day, the family's basement looked like either a miniature geology lab or a prison rock pile. His prize "find" was the fifteen-pound onyx elephant he lugged through a long trip and back home on an airplane. One day, when each child officially moves out, we can present him with all of his valuables we have carefully saved!

8. Provide Responsible Guidance and Supervision

RESPONSIBLE PARENTING DICTATES supervision, either ours or that of someone we trust. Jimmy likes to construct toy swords and play with caps and cap guns. Josh wants to make "explosives." There is a big difference. *We need to know what our children are doing.* Although it is important to be in touch (by telephone or e-mail) if we cannot be where

> "We parents are the holders of a priceless gift, a gift we received from countless generations we never knew, a gift that only we now possess and only we can give to our children. That unique gift, of course, is the gift of ourselves."
>
> —Fred Rogers and Barry Head,
> *Mister Rogers Talks with Parents*
> (Pittsburgh: Family Communications, 1983), p. 256

they are, even school-age children can get into trouble without a responsible person actually on-site. Part of being a parent is paying close attention to our children's activities and using the prerogative to redirect them. We do not have to participate in their actions to understand what they are doing. With growing children, there is no substitute for being there.

Some activities require appropriate space and safety measures. Since he was very young, Art was enticed by the small backyard shed but had never been allowed to climb onto it. Finally, at nine, he and his friends were permitted to explore its possibilities. They spent a great deal of time perching on the shed's roof and devising ways to jump off. Elated, they rigged a garden hose to a tree as a sliding pole and used it for raising and lowering themselves. All afternoon, they invented descents from the shed. Within an age-appropriate environment of comfort and safety, a child can enjoy certain freedoms. A responsible adult's job is to ensure the comfort and safety; our children will supply the freedom.

As we uncover and support each child's abilities, our focus is on the child herself. *It is the child who is important to us, not her accomplishments.* "If a child comes to be valued too much for what she has achieved or whether she has met certain goals dictated by a program, rather than for what she is,"[4] she feels diminished as a person. Supporting her strengths, we can nurture her emotionally—our most important job.

TIPS TO TRY

A. Appreciate Individuality
   Allow choices in:
   > clothing styles or colors, arrangement of personal belongings, and private space.

B. Respect Choices
   Listen to his music.
   Admire his projects.
   Offer:
   > magazines, tapes, and library books of his choice.

C. Encourage Interests
   Offer:
   > supplies (markers, clay, athletic equipment, bins of fabric or wood scraps, blocks), transportation, shared activities, and outings.

D. Stimulate New Interests
   Encourage exploration by:
   > letting children try new things in new places, such as hands-on activities at nature centers or museums.

E. Support Activities
   Listen, encourage, or observe:
   > recitals, sports events, and plays.

F. Allow Changes
   When children change their minds:
   > discuss reasons and offer alternatives.

G. Accept a Unique Pace
   Begin lessons and structured activities when children:
   > show a particular interest, maintain a sustained interest, and are (developmentally) ready.

H. Provide Responsible Guidance and Supervision
   Ensure:
   > a safe environment, workable rules, and a trusted caregiver.

3

On the Lookout

SANDY: STEPHEN, AT six, always had a lot of stories in his head. A sedentary child, he began writing about what he knew best. One story featured a boy whose mother (me!) "made him go outside to play." He created comic books filled with drawings and, later, science fiction stories and short plays. As a young adult, he has selected poetry and literary criticism as his career. Given options, Stephen always chose to write.

Every child is born with his own strengths and unique qualities.[1] As parents, we can see our children developing choices. Even two-year-olds show preferences. John loved solitary play, building intricate structures for hours. Holly and her band of playmates relished knocking down everything in their paths. Children play differently; it is up to us to pay attention.

> Every child is born with his own strengths and unique qualities.

Observing our children in their different activities, we can quickly see their special qualities. Any parent can confirm that no two siblings have the same personalities, even if

30

they have similar interests and abilities. Each requires a different kind of support. Children thrive when their environment supports their style.[2] A quiet, reserved child feels overwhelmed in a boisterous setting. An artistic child becomes frustrated when she is expected to conform to restrictive standards. What should we watch for?

1. Would my child rather throw a ball or watch a ball game? (active/sedentary)

2. Is she happier alone, one-on-one, or with a group? (solitary/sociable)

3. Does he like to take charge or prefer to follow the leader? (leading/following)

4. Would she rather listen to a story or look at the pictures? (auditory/visual)

5. Would he rather cook the food or develop new recipes? (concrete/theoretical)

6. Does my child prefer to follow instructions for games or create her own rules? (orderly/creative)

To identify their strengths, we need to recognize how children function. One of the easiest methods is just to watch them (even for short periods) as they play alone or with others. How do they approach a task? When constructing a block building, for instance, do they first notice what their playmates are doing, or do they plunge right in? When frustrated, do they ask for adult assistance, or do they want to work it out for themselves? Over a period of several weeks of brief observations, what characteristics stand out? When asked, what do our children think they are good at? Children concentrate on the things they enjoy the most. The child who likes to draw or play with puzzles prob-

> "It is only as a child's . . . uniqueness is respected that he can permit his individuality to unfold."

ably has a strong sense of design and well-developed small-muscle coordination. The child who never met a tree he could not climb and hangs by his heels from the top of the jungle gym usually has a well-developed sense of balance and highly skilled use of his body in space.

By elementary school, every child displays "areas of strength, personality traits, topics of interest, and specific skills that parents can identify and help develop."[3]

Linda: For Cliff, dinner time was show time. From the age of six, Cliff punctuated the family meal with hilarious renditions of television commercials. By fourth grade, he was learning to recite famous monologues, and in fifth grade, he played the role of Patrick—the only child's part—in a community theater production of Auntie Mame.

In another family, eight-year-old Jeannette was regularly gathering the neighborhood children at the foot of the sliding board in her backyard for half an hour of storytelling.

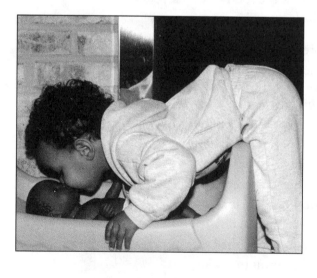

They enjoyed their story time almost as much as their "teacher" did. Jeannette began to hone her leadership skills right in her own backyard. Cliff's family was his first and most important audience; his feeling of success at home enabled him to perform in front of others. "It is only as a child's . . . uniqueness is respected that he can permit his individuality to unfold."[4]

From Howard Gardner's "theory of multiple intelligences" to Robert Sternberg's "three types of basic intelligence," researchers have categorized learning styles. No one person falls exclusively into any single style; we each operate in a combination of ways. When we help clarify for ourselves and identify

"Find something that you are attracted to, and let that energy draw you."

—James Earl Jones, actor,
interview with authors, June 22, 1998

for our children some of their developing strengths, we are building the foundations for their self-esteem. "The child with self-confidence surges ahead to develop his particular potentials and talents."[5]

The characteristics used here consolidate our own findings into user-friendly terms for parents. In the interest of simplicity, we categorize some easily recognized behaviors. These may be helpful as general guidelines to understanding children's preferences. *To find out how children function best, parents need to know what they enjoy most.*

1. Active/Sedentary

BOTH ACTIVE AND sedentary children need encouragement, and both need physical outlets. Keith was on every school team; there was no sport he did not like. Hank went to every game, marching up and down the sidelines to cheer the players. Supporting the team was his sport. Both boys were physically active, but in very different ways. Some children are born with excellent physical skills. When we watch these children play, we can see that, like Keith, they run faster, kick farther, throw and catch more accurately than their playmates. Others, like Hank, relish physical activity without displaying the same skills. They might like the excitement of leading cheers, carrying heavy athletic equipment for the team, riding a bike, swinging, or climbing trees.

Also in need of such outlets are sedentary children who are not as comfortable using their bodies. It is up to us as parents to give these children such a wide variety of choices that they can find something physical that they naturally enjoy. Shana, who could sit quietly reading a book for hours, found to her surprise that she liked gliding down a snowy

slope on skis. Joellen, an introspective amateur naturalist, was encouraged to take weekend hikes to pursue her hobby.

Sedentary is not necessarily solitary. The spectators among us could enjoy such activities as collecting baseball cards and tabulating player statistics. Instead of sports, they might enjoy reading, sewing, or writing. Children who enjoy working on student publications, playing board games, or working together on a city of Legos are finding social satisfaction through nonphysical activity.

As we now know, a child's long-term physical health requires some regular physical activity. We do our children a service when we help them discover something active they can enjoy, while continuing to respect their preference for sedentary over physical pursuits. How frequently our child is physically active is up to her; *our job is to provide her with ideas and opportunities.*

2. Solitary/Sociable

ALTHOUGH *ALL* CHILDREN need social experiences, some also require a greater amount of time alone than others. Eric and Scott were at it again, in a brawling heap on Scott's bedroom floor. While nine-year-old Scott was laboriously sorting his shell collection, six-year-old Eric, knocking furiously and getting no response, dove into the room, upsetting his brother's careful layout. All Eric wanted was a playmate. His social brother sought constant companionship, but Scott just wanted to work on his projects alone. With group activities and lots of play dates for Eric, peace was more easily established. Scott's parents carefully planned some interactive activities for him with just one friend at a time, and he was able to have other periods for quiet pursuits.

Children who prefer projects requiring precision and order usually require undisturbed time. Ten-year-old Harriet was a wonderful doll maker. She made dolls out of toothpicks and old wooden clothespins; she designed and made their clothing out of paper and scraps of fabric. With the tiniest paintbrush she created features for their faces. The one thing she could not use was the company of her five-year-old brother. However, her friend Penny sometimes came over, and the two girls worked side by side on their individual dolls. The presence of this one friend was comfortable for Harriet.

Children might use companionship in different ways. The child who is constantly testing his abilities might seek competitive settings (team or group games, debates, artistic or scholastic competitions) to stimulate his talents. Alexander loved to run. He was delighted when he was finally old enough to try out for the track team. He enjoyed the daily practices and routines he shared with his friends but relished the weekly meets where he had the chance to compete. Instead of just suggesting he run around his neighborhood, Alexander's parents had found him a setting that also fulfilled his need for competition. Whenever possible, they went to his meets.

> Allowing children their different social styles helps reinforce their developing talents.

Cooperative endeavors attract children who value group input and shared responsibilities as well as shared rewards ("playing house," building forts, organizing social events).

Linda: Beginning at about eleven, Cliff loved organizing birthday parties for his younger brother. He designed beanbag games, relay races, and yelled encouragement to all the participants. In college, a sympathetic adviser for younger students, he became a peer counselor, who scrounged extra seating for his dorm room to make it more inviting. His empathy revealed his strong interpersonal abilities.

Allowing children their different social styles helps reinforce their developing talents. The child who is surrounded with playmates may be refining his negotiating skills; the solitary one may be writing poetry.

3. Leading/Following

ON A COLLEGE admissions application, a candidate reluctantly replied to a question on leadership that she, in fact, was a follower. A prompt acceptance letter congratulated her: "'We are especially happy to have you, since in next year's class we will have four hundred students: Three hundred ninety-nine leaders and one follower.'"[6] Every community needs leaders *and* followers.

Observing children over time in group activities, we can see the roles in which they are most comfortable. We can also support their need to try out different roles with their peers. Wesley, at nine, is well liked by his classmates. His close friends tend to be strong leaders who rely on his support. When he voices an opinion, they listen. In her group, ten-year-old Ashley is the organizer. She is the one people look to for ideas and direction. Leaders can be such strong, directive personalities as Ashley or quiet role models who draw other children to them. Like Wesley, followers can be attentive listeners and valuable contributors.

Children assume leadership roles in connection with specific interest areas: one might manage the fund-raising project for the Chess Club; another organizes a class trip; a third serves as student conductor for a school musical. Renee, a quiet, reflective fifteen-year-old, asserted her artistic talent when she courageously applied for the position of art editor on the high school yearbook staff. Her work impressed everyone, and she was stimulated to develop her skills by applying for, and earning, a scholarship to a highly regarded art school. When they have an opportunity to *exercise* leadership skills, children find to their surprise that they *have* them!

4. Auditory/Visual

A CHILD MIGHT prefer either auditory or visual responses to relate to his surroundings. Eight-year-old Zachary did not like to see the pictures in the storybooks his mother read him. "The ones in my head are better," he said. In time, he was able to put down the "ones in [his] head" as he began to weave his own beautiful tapestries through his words. He became a talented creative writer. Four-year-old Juanita did not like others to read aloud to her; she wanted to "read" the pictures herself. She developed a preference for certain kinds of illustrations and began to draw and paint. At an early age, she had a highly developed sense of color and design. Both of these children were allowed to express and develop their preferences.

Those who love conversation, music, and languages display an auditory bent. Although writing is a concrete visual act, writers also have strong auditory awareness. They are impassioned with language—its sounds and its meanings. They have words in their heads and assimilate their experiences in terms of language. Stephen at twenty-four was taking a trip

"To help a young artist, support his effort and be willing to accept the surprises of its outcome."

—Robert Henri,
The Art Spirit (Philadelphia: Lippincott, 1960)

abroad. He did not need a camera, he explained, because he was "writing it all down."

Children who love to read maps, work puzzles, and put together models show a visual orientation.

Sandy: *Daniel has always loved movies and television. From the time he was a toddler, he put together complicated puzzles. At three, he gave adult drivers accurate directions to locations across town, from his car seat. Now that he is a young adult, his bedroom reflects his concentration on visual appeal. Large plants, surrealist art posters, and a rusty metal sculpture punctuate the contrasts of his black-and-white color scheme. In college, he studied visual arts. He takes his camera everywhere.*

Many of us come with a combination of visual and auditory preferences.

Linda: *My husband Barry enjoys music and has a beautiful tenor voice. He has performed in choral programs and loves going to the opera, with its majestic music and elaborate visual displays. When time permits, he creates intriguing metal sculptures in his garage-studio. His lively work decorates our house and yard.*

Like Barry, *children have preferences and characteristics ranging along a spectrum in any category.* It is not necessary to pigeonhole them, just to watch what they choose to do.

5. Concrete/Theoretical

CHILDREN WHO SPEND time formulating ideas might be less comfortable with their concrete representations. Stuart, a theoretical thinker, would be instantly discharged from any infantry unit. Upon being directed, "Over the hill, men!" he would respond thoughtfully, "Perhaps it would be better to go around the hill or move several battalions through the stream or set up an encampment in the woods until dark." In addition, he would have a great deal of difficulty locating his combat boots. His brother Avery, however, would have everyone organized into columns, complete with all necessary gear, well in advance of departure. Even within the same family, children operate in their own individual ways.

Brant, a gifted young scientist, was a teaching assistant at a large university. During labs, his students always sat in the back; it was safer there. Brant was well known for accidentally breaking and exploding his materials. Such theoretical thinkers as Stuart and Brant often see patterns or interrelationships as they constantly analyze their world; however, they need someone around to find their socks! Concrete thinkers, on the other hand, are practical and comfortable in hands-on situations. They might have less interest in the *reasons* for things; they just want to *do* them.

A concrete problem solver is undeterred by a lack of information. Roger loved strawberries, so he planted his very own strawberry plants in his backyard. Squirrels love strawberries, too, he discovered. So he began to research methods to discourage strawberry thieves. He proudly announced to his parents that he had found several solutions. "We need to sprinkle dried fox urine in my garden!" he recommended. "Or we could just buy a flesh-eating animal that will eat the squirrels!" In this case, the research turned out to be as exciting as the gardening. Pursuing concrete solutions, such problem solvers have a clear focus on their goals but might have creative ways of achieving them.

6. Orderly/Creative

RULES AND REGULATIONS form a comforting framework for children who think and respond in an orderly way. They thrive within the security of a structured environment, where the rules are clear and predictable. They enjoy a setting where they know what their schedule will be and what to expect in most situations. Other children need the freedom to pioneer. They like to have choices for their activities, frequently balking at constraints of time and other limitations. They need the adventure of finding new ways to approach situations. The child who can happily play Monopoly for hours might function securely in a regulated environment; her companion might only enjoy the game by creating novel ways to beat the system.

Priscilla needed to have order—school materials, clothing, and a routine that followed a precise pattern each day. Predictability made her comfortable. Her parents helped her develop organizational skills for academic work and her daily schedule. She grew up to be a community activist who also managed a religious education program. She adeptly ran a household that required geographic relocations every three years.

Roz had strong opinions about how things should be done. She hated schedules and complained about soccer's regimentation; she did not want to follow the rules—she wanted to make up her own. Because she genuinely enjoyed the physical activity and her teammates, her parents encouraged her to stay with her sport. As a teenager, she coached a younger team. She was pleased with the flexibility of (finally!) being in charge. Observing how our children respond to everyday situations, we can recognize patterns that reveal their styles.

"The gift of fantasy has meant more to me than my talent for absorbing positive knowledge."

—Albert Einstein,
cited in Thomas Armstrong,
Awakening Your Child's Natural Genius: Enhancing Curiosity, Creativity, and Learning Ability (New York: Putnam's, 1991), p. 188

Sometimes adults, thinking in a practical manner, see things in a totally different way from their creative children.

Linda: During one of our summer camping trips, my family spent an afternoon visiting the Crooked River Dowel Factory, near Papoose Pond. A sea of wooden dowels engulfed the grounds. The best part was that visitors could take as many of the flawed dowels as they could carry away. Barry saw this as a major source of firewood for our family's campfire, which was both stove and heat source for the week-long Maine vacation. So everyone—Barry and I, our sons, Roy and Cliff, and even the accompanying grandparents—helped load up every possible cranny of the family station wagon with dowels.

The next morning after breakfast, Roy, four, and Cliff, two, set to work. They saw the load of dowels through entirely different eyes than their parents. For hours, they worked quietly, dashing back and forth from car to campsite with armloads of dowels. These splintery sticks of wood became the fulfillment of a fantasy for two eager little boys who built themselves a "log" fort. We enjoyed watching.

With creative children, parents can expect the unexpected.

Sandy: Daniel played guitar, among other instruments. When he first got his guitar case, I insisted that he label it so it would not be confused with someone else's case. He made sure it was clearly his. Instead of attaching a label with his name, Daniel turned the entire case into a colorful painting of a howling face. He fulfilled my directive in his unique style.

When a child believes in herself, she is free to explore her ideas and deviate from the norms she observes around her. Sometimes youngsters are ostracized or belittled by their peers because they see things "differently." Too often, teachers fail to encourage them or support their efforts. Although they often threaten the status quo, it is creative thinkers who move society forward.

As much as a child's environment influences him, he also influences his environment.[7] *When a child exhibits particular strengths or interests, even as an infant, he is giving signals to his*

When we attend to a child's interests, we see patterns evolve.

Linda: *When four-year-old Roy climbed into my lap and asked, "I know you and Daddy made me, but how did you get the bones inside?" he was just beginning a lifelong fascination with the sciences. Through library books, magazine articles, occasional visits to museums and nature centers, and summer camping trips, his wonder and interests grew. Science fair projects, summer science programs, and high school and college fellowships in medical research led to his current medical career. Even though he does not sit in my lap anymore, he still asks a lot of questions.*

parents. A physically active baby thrives in surroundings that are safe and inviting to explore; he loves to climb over, under, and into boxes, furniture, and play equipment. As a result, his parents ensure that he has ready access to this kind of setting, if only by blocking off part of a living room or back-yard. His preferences have dictated his environment, which, in turn, has stimulated further development of his abilities.

We reduce a child's frustration when we provide for his needs. When it was clear that James did not enjoy competitive sports, his parents found him drama groups, sculpture classes, and a lot of playtime with his friends. When Keith did not enjoy music lessons, his parents did not force him to continue; they respected his wish to be physically active. He plays a team sport each season. *The support, encouragement, and nourishment offered by parents as mentors is a determining factor in the development of a child's talents.* Once we understand our children's abilities, we can more easily sustain them.

TIPS TO TRY

A. Active children like:
   space to move in; daily physical activity; and frequent
   opportunities to climb, run, and throw a ball.
   Active children need:
   a period of quiet time each day to recharge.
B. Sedentary children like:
   reading, collecting, playing board games, creating art
   projects, and listening to music.
   Sedentary children need:
   noncompetitive physical opportunities (such as
   swimming, hiking, skiing, roller skating).
C. Solitary children like:
   private time to work on projects, read, write, practice
   an instrument, or daydream.
   Solitary children need:
   interaction with similar peers in one-to-one situations or
   small groups.
D. Sociable children like:
   group settings, constant playmates, cooperative
   activities, and competitive activities.
   Sociable children need:
   some quiet time each day to think, play, and rest.
E. Leaders like:
   working in a group environment, having opportunities to
   organize people, and managing activities.
   Leaders need:
   to listen to other people's opinions and ideas.
F. Followers like:
   supporting others, receiving concrete direction,
   and having appreciative peers.
   Followers need:
   opportunities to be heard and settings where they
   are valued.
G. Auditory children like:
   music, languages, oral directions, conversation,
   public speaking, and acting.
   Auditory children need:
   opportunities to perform, communicate, and listen to
   what they choose.

TIPS TO TRY

(CONTINUED)

H. Visual children like:
     maps, puzzles, models, movies, art projects, comic
     books, museums, photography, and sight-seeing.
     Visual children need:
     interesting things to look at, manipulate, and enjoy
     (their clothing, rooms, possessions).

I. Concrete thinkers like:
     clear instruction, specific goals, practical approaches,
     and hands-on opportunities.
     Concrete thinkers need:
     to encounter open-ended ideas (ask "What if . . . ?")
     and use their imaginations.

J. Theoretical thinkers like:
     analysis, patterns, or interrelationships; few time
     constraints; and freedom to explore their ideas.
     Theoretical thinkers need:
     daily schedules to count on.

K. Orderly children like:
     predictable schedules, clear rules, logical conse-
     quences, and an organized physical environment.
     Orderly children need:
     to tolerate other people's ways of doing things.

L. Creative children like:
     freedom to find their own solutions, tolerance of their
     unique style, few limits, and a variety of materials to use.
     Creative children need:
     supportive (not restrictive) structure for their everyday
     schedules.

4

Enriched and Fortified

A DRIENNE, TEN, WAS doing her homework for a unit on nutrition in her science class. She had to keep track of all the food she ate for twenty-four hours. When she tallied up the number of fruits, vegetables, meats, and carbohydrates she had eaten, she marched over to the refrigerator and poured herself a glass of milk. Her mother watched with some astonishment, because her daughter disliked milk. Finishing with a wide milk mustache, Adrienne looked up grinning. "Now I'm perfect!" she announced.

Essential Ingredients

WE GREW UP hearing about the bread that "builds strong bodies eight ways." "Enriched and fortified" children are built with at least seven essential ingredients:

1. Parents who provide their time

2. A stimulating home environment

3. Time and space to explore

4. Experiences that foster expanding interests

5. Physical resources

6. Someone to share their enthusiasms

7. Opportunities for success and failure

As with the finest fare, the best ingredients are often the simplest. In the case of parenting, they are also often the closest at hand.

Because of the prevalence of dual-career and single-parent families and the demanding nature of both adults' jobs and children's activities, a kind of "time poverty" has developed in our culture.[1] Our lifestyles encourage us to substitute *things* for *people*. We may rationalize that we are showing our love by giving our children "the things we never had" and experiences intended to "enrich" them. What we often forget is that "to a child, love is spelled: *t - i - m - e*."[2]

1. Parents Who Provide Their Time

FROM THEIR EARLIEST years, when we babble back at our babies, we are communicating the importance of language. When we talk "*with* our children, not *at* them," we begin an exchange that will help them develop language and enhance their self-esteem.[3] Time to answer questions, to find out about a child's day, to consider what children are doing and thinking about is a way to make a child begin to understand that her opinions are important. *No matter how crowded our personal schedule, a special time each day, set aside for each child, sends a strong message.* It helps her feel special, unique, and valued. When she senses her

One of the few lasting gifts that parents can give is the "gift of themselves."

"**A** child needs to talk; a parent needs to *be there* to listen. Time spent with a child is important. It bolsters his confidence in himself."

—Ruth M. Cass, artist,
interview with authors, June 2, 1998

importance to us, she feels important to herself. She learns to share. A child who experiences special time with a parent is more likely to allow others the same.[4]

A family that makes a habit of spending time together can boost the self-esteem of each of its members. Working on a family project, playing a game, or spending a day seeing sights together helps build a closeness that comes from shared experiences. Time at home on a regular basis, whenever and however we fit it in, is a significant component of family unity. The expectation that some family members will be at home most evenings, if at all possible, can make the family setting a reliable, predictable environment for a child. He knows that he can count on his family to be around. A child feels accountable only to an adult who is really *there*, not one whose attention or physical presence is elsewhere.[5] *Even as teenagers, children get the message that they are valued when parents put limits on their own time away from home, especially during the school week.*

Regular mealtimes are good settings for family discussion or decision making. They are appropriate times to involve teens, who spend less time in the house than younger children, in the dynamics of the family. Can everyone be home for dinner most nights? Or for breakfast most mornings? Or to share a special breakfast or lunch each Saturday? When adults model respectful listening, children follow. We might be surprised and delighted at the ingenuity and insight of our children's ideas. When children are involved and respected in a family's decision making, the confidence they feel can carry over into other areas. The family cheering section has given many children the support they needed to pursue their goals.

When parents value their children's interests, their support can become contagious; other family members sometimes join in.

Sandy: Andrew is the only one of our four sons to enjoy sports. When he was six years old and just beginning soccer, he was nervous that he would not be as skilled as some of his other teammates whose families valued and played sports more frequently. One of the season's first games was played early on a cool Saturday morning, when his oldest brother, Stephen, just happened to be home from college. At kick-off Andrew looked up to find his bleary-eyed brother cheering him on from the sidelines. Now a confident veteran player, Andrew still wishes someone in the family understood the game, but he is proud when any older brother asks about his game and when he spots us on the sidelines.

In Bloom's study of exceptionally high-achieving adults, their parents had willingly rearranged their schedules to accommodate their children's activities.[6] In a family with two or more children, parents have the interests and needs of more than one child to take into account. Caring parents can be flexible but also need to be realistic. Recognizing that each child deserves our attention, it is up to us to juggle schedules and arrangements, finding ways that work for our families. One of the few lasting gifts that parents can give is the "gift of themselves."[7]

Bedtimes can be effectively used as special times for a child and parent to be alone. With the commotion of the day at its final ebb, the quiet of the night can be a time to share ideas, feelings, fears, and hopes. Even a brief period of time that a child can count on at the end of his day is special. Sometimes a review of the day will bring out a child's hidden concerns; sometimes a story read and discussed will lead to broader issues. One child loved to read humor books aloud to her dad; another liked to discuss events in the news; another enjoyed poetry, from Shel Silverstein to Edgar Allen Poe. Even when he was a capable reader, Ian enjoyed his father's nightly rendition of a small portion of *A Tale of Two Cities.* Sometimes ideas or problems seem to come up "out of the blue" at these times. However brief, a parent's undivided time can lead the child to explore alternatives, identify central issues, and evaluate possible solutions. Critical thinking seems best fostered in a supportive setting. *A child's comfort with adult conversation begins by conversing with his own parents.*

Special time with a child can be used for encouragement of her abilities. Our time sitting or working in the room where a child is practicing, being physically available to help with a project, view or read a report, makes a child feel that what he does counts.

What we choose to spend our time on is also of interest to our children. Community involvement, sports, or the arts are areas our children can find interesting and stimulating. Bringing family donations to a community shelter, going for a Saturday morning jog, or putting together a family newsletter are things even young children can understand and

"There are times in all children's development when they need parents more rather than less. We've got to provide more cushioning for parents so they can be available when their child needs them."

—T. Berry Brazelton,
interview with authors, January 25, 1999

> "Through my grandmother [Rose Kennedy], I learned that you were expected to make a commitment to the greater community, using whatever skills you had."
>
> —The Honorable Mark Shriver, state congressional delegate (D-Maryland), interview with authors, July 8, 1998

enjoy. *When we give them a chance to participate in activities important to us, we tell children* they *are important, too.* When we direct our energy to the community beyond ourselves, we demonstrate the value of selflessness and encourage our children to use their talents in the service of others. By our choices, we acknowledge our priorities.

2. A Stimulating Home Environment

CHILDREN ARE INSPIRED when they are surrounded by alluring things.

Linda: Our young niece and nephew love to visit their Uncle Barry's house. From the moment they get out of their car, they see the colorful metal sculptures moving in the breeze. In the front hall, they are greeted by a life-sized suit of armor and a collection of colorful masks on the walls. Bright mobiles, paintings, and blooming plants decorate the rooms. The kids are fascinated by the newt and toad in their tanks and the squirrels and wild rabbits that sometimes roam the backyard. There is a pond filled with frogs, water lilies, a fountain, and goldfish. No wonder both children enjoy their visits.

The backdrop for an enriched and fortified child is an enriched home environment. But we do not have to have suits of armor; posters, collections, and souvenirs provide the same visual excitement. We do not need a grand piano to hear music; a tape recorder or radio can provide similar enrichment. Children can create their own artwork. When children's work is on display, they feel pride.

In a stimulating setting, children are seen and heard doing all sorts of marvelously creative things. They are busy "running, play-acting, building, drawing, conversing, writing, experimenting, reading, exploring, wondering, laughing, and in many other ways, vigorously interacting with the world."[8] Of course, to comfortably promote this kind of activity, parents have to childproof their home. A safe child has room to grow and explore; most pediatricians' offices provide pamphlets with childproofing tips. When we give children opportunities to exercise their curiosity, we "don't build walls; [we] open doors."[9] Instead of courses or kits, children need freedom to be themselves in a world they can explore.[10]

> "Don't build walls; open doors."

Home-grown creativity includes providing materials and opportunities. For example, everyone in Sarah's family produces original cards for special occasions. If the Hallmark cards company depended on Sarah's family for business, it would go bankrupt. In Chad's family, Halloween costumes are always homemade. One October, Chad spent days constructing a haunted house outfit that would come alive when he wore it. He covered his face with white makeup and wore long white gloves; various noises emanated from inside his cardboard box, and bats and skeletons swung from its windows. When he completed work on his haunted house costume, his eyes sparkled. Youngsters use their creativity to express their ideas.

Some children will create music on any available surface, whether it's pot and pan lids or an electronic keyboard. Others need to move, climbing over, crawling under, throwing, running, or jumping. They explore language, asking questions, making rhymes, reading stories, and writing journals. Their homemade clay sculptures, wooden goblets, and framed original poems can be prominently displayed treasures from each of our children. When they see their creations on exhibit, children realize how much they are valued.

We can stimulate appreciation for language by encouraging our children to ask questions and by asking questions ourselves. Eight-year-old Ari was asked how he would redesign his room. His eyes lit up. Remembering his tour of a submarine, he described wood-paneled walls with drop-down bunks, equipment that slid out of walls at the touch of a button, and lots of ropes to climb on. Such open-ended questions teach youngsters that there are not always set answers; they also learn that everything they wish for does not necessarily come true! When we model independent thinking,we help our children trust what they have to offer. Although we cannot always provide them with their dream bedrooms, we can show them their dreams are important.

Our interactions with our children set the tone for their relationships with others. Skills that enable children to listen, share, and focus on other people give them the tools for successful interactions. How *we* handle disagreement, frustration, problem solving, and getting along with others is absorbed by our children. Our home can be a welcoming oasis for them and their friends. We might even ask how we can make it more inviting. When they feel important in the family, they become confident in their dealings with others.

Young people love to hear stories about themselves from parents or grandparents. We can expand their awareness by sharing bits of family history, photos, and heirlooms. Special interest might center on a family member for whom they

"The greatest gift that parents can give is unconditional love."

—Chris Wallace,
ABC News correspondent, interview with authors, June 11, 1998

have been named or one who had exciting adventures. Such personalized history can promote enthusiasm about history in general.

Sandy: *We were recently at a newsstand when a special book caught Andrew's eye. It was a compilation of* Life *magazine news stories from 1923 through 1998. "I'd like to buy that for Grandma," he announced. "That's her whole lifetime!" His grandmother loved her present and could not wait for him to come visit and go over her memories of some of the historic events pictured.*

> If we treat our children "as if they already are what they are capable of becoming," we give inspiration for further growth.

Parents can provide different kinds of encouragement. Most significant is unconditional love, regardless of our children's strengths or weaknesses. We acknowledge the obstacles they have had to overcome in reaching a goal. We appreciate and applaud specific accomplishments. More valuable and realistic to a child than the statement "Oh, you're a great gymnast" would be "That cartwheel on the balance beam was exciting to watch!" If we treat our children "as if *they already are what they are capable of becoming,*" we inspire further growth.[11]

Sometimes risk taking deserves our support; we want our children to be confident enough to venture into new fields and accept new challenges. Estelle, most comfortable behind the scenes, was encouraged by her mom to audition for the school play. She surprised everyone, including herself, with a hilarious performance in the comedy's leading role. Parents can contribute to mental imaging in either positive or negative ways. When we say "don't," the child has a mental picture of doing what the parent advised against, and often that picture then comes true. The flip side is a positive idea: "Hit that ball a mile!" The child has a mental image of succeeding.[12] An accepting and nonjudgmental home environment encourages a child's self-esteem and creativity.

To be creative, a child must be inner directed; he must follow the inclinations of his own choosing. He might ask odd questions, think and act differently, and solve problems with unusual solutions.

Sandy: When he was sixteen, Daniel was assigned to write a persuasive speech for his English class. His response was to write and perform an original musical composition extolling the virtues of the mandolin. Accustomed to his originality, we appreciated his efforts; fortunately, his teachers did, too.

Parents who listen to and accept their children's ideas inspire independent and creative thought. Creativity requires the ability to take risks and to accept the results. "Creativity takes courage."[13]

"**C**reativity takes courage."

Exploring their world without relying on a house full of toys provides children the option of relying on their own inventiveness for stimulation. Even if children are messy, disorganized, and not concerned with adult approval, they often have dreams and goals that should be encouraged.

Responsible parents teach children to make decisions and set their own goals. We can offer suggestions, explain the consequences of the alternatives, and allow our youngsters to learn decision making for themselves. Capable children often have lofty aspirations and find it difficult to be realistic in their expectations. Instead of being overwhelmed by big goals, they can be taught to break them down into manageable segments and take them one at a time.

Young people feel more effective when they learn to use tools to help organize their lives. Calendars, planning books, and memo boards can give them the aids they need for order. In Ellie's house, a giant family calendar hangs on the kitchen wall, with smaller bulletin boards nearby for each child. On hers, Ellie keeps track of her student government meetings, play rehearsals, soccer practices, and piano lessons and can make her own arrangements to be where she has to go. She can keep herself organized. Our principal goal as parents is to raise children to be in charge of themselves.

3. Time and Space to Explore

"I'M GOING TO have *my* quiet time, and you're going to have *your* quiet time," Lindsay told her two-year-old, Robin, "and I'm not coming out of my room for an hour!" She left her in her own room, with the door open but the child gate secured across the doorway. We all need quiet time. An enriched child is given the freedom to rely on her own resources and some time to just "mess around." A child who can entertain herself is never bored. In her own time and space, a child uses her imagination, develops new ideas, and gets to know herself. Even a social child can benefit from the satisfaction of her own company. When a child does not have to account for her private time and space, she can feel comfortable to be herself. She can be her own best friend.

No matter what kind of home he lives in, each child needs a space of his own. Here he can "work on projects, store collections, keep special possessions, and maintain some personal clutter."[14] In her touching book *Evan's Corner,* Elizabeth Starr Hill writes of a little boy whose family lives in a very cramped apartment. To make her children feel special, Evan's mother allows each to choose his or her own corner as a special spot. In her private space, a child learns to understand her rights and others' needs. By acknowledging the importance of a child's personal space and time without evaluation or intrusion, parents demonstrate respect.

"Toys must be *interactive*, not preprogrammed, for a child to grow."

—Debra Aaron, owner, ZZToys,
Fernandina Beach, Florida, interview with authors, October 25, 1998

4. Experiences That Foster Expanding Interests

WHEN WE GIVE our children outside experiences, we remind them of the enrichment available beyond their homes. Buddy's family likes bird watching. They have a library of bird books that Buddy uses to help identify visitors to his backyard birdfeeders. On their weekend walks, he, his little sister, and his parents all eagerly look for specimens. Shel's family enjoys art. Their visits to museums included each child bringing along his own sketchbook. Years later, the youngest and the oldest children have found they share similar artistic taste, and they enjoy going to museums together. The outcome of these exposures can be the long-term benefits of companionship, enjoyment of mutual interests, and discovery of new interests.

To expose children to new experiences, we can begin by sharing whatever we most enjoy. If we like theater, we can take our sons or daughters to performances; if we love to hike, children can come along. When they get older, children reveal their own interests, and the whole family can benefit. Tim, eleven, became enamored of Revolutionary War history and now has his whole family in tow, visiting reenactments all dressed in period costumes. We are surrounded by a wealth of people, events, and places. Nature offers a sense of calm for adults and children. Tramping through the fall leaves, spotting the first spring buds, or watching the heavens reminds us that when we slow down, we see most clearly. Children who are attuned to what is outside themselves can become inspired to explore what lies within.

Giving children the opportunity to discuss experiences enhances their learning. When we let them "stretch," to experience concerts, poetry, science demonstrations, and sports, we encourage them to grow. With a small amount of his own savings, Anton, ten, invested in a stock of his choice. Whenever the morning paper arrived, he laid first claim to the business section and followed the market's fluctuations. When his father came home each evening, they spread out the stock pages and reviewed them together.

Communities offer many opportunities for stimulation. From after-school courses in cooking or printmaking to community ice skating or hockey teams, little theater, and service clubs, a full spectrum of activity is available. Sometimes involvement comes through friends, neighbors, or even baby-sitters. At age eleven, Peter's favorite activity was watching television. One evening, his baby-sitter asked him whether he would be willing to help her with a project. Involved with an opera company in their city, she was looking for youngsters to serve as supernumeraries, or "supers," in a particular performance. "Opera?" he said incredulously, but he went with her out of curiosity. He became a super. With Peter onstage as a spear holder, his family was drawn to attend. So began his family's discovery—and love—of the opera. A child's new activity can entice and enrich the whole family.

Children can also learn to donate time and skills to others. Teenagers, especially, can begin by identifying a problem they would like to help solve. As they help others, they discover that "opinions do not make problems disappear, but commitments do."[15] A religious framework reinforces selflessness. Within a faith community, numerous skills can blossom: leadership, social skills, public speaking ability, musical and artistic talent. Churches, synagogues, community centers, and other public spaces that promote a child's artistic, musical, or performance abilities reinforce and inspire her efforts. Like many other musicians, Aretha Franklin got her start as a child singing in her own church.

5. Physical Resources

PHYSICAL RESOURCES ARE essential ingredients for our children as they grow. At six, Pablo's favorite gifts are collections of batteries, wires, and wood and metal scraps that he can forge into his own creations. For Megan, any log, barrel, fence, or ladder provides a satisfying outlet for physical activity; a trip to the local playground is a special outing. From gardening tools to microscopes, from balls to cookbooks, children need physical "handles" to connect them to their environment. An active child should have space and opportunity to throw a ball, roll on the floor, climb, slide, swim, dance, or skate. A less physically active youngster might enjoy collecting shells, leaves, rocks, stamps, or coins. Books and periodicals enrich any child's interests. A magazine subscription in her own name can be a special gift.

Even for young children, written materials are valuable. Research suggests that parents who read and write notes to youngsters increase their children's ability to read and write.[16] One summer, Catherine's family decided to keep journals. The children, ages five, seven, and nine, each worked on their own entries daily. In some cases the children drew pictures to tell their stories, and in some cases the older ones wrote (or dictated to a parent or caregiver) long narratives. By summer's end, the family had a wonderful record of each person's perspectives.

> A good toy is a "catalyst, a means rather than an end."

Reading aloud should continue, even after children can read by themselves, for as long as they are willing to sit and listen. Good stories can be problem-solving experiences. When children examine how a conflict is dealt with, they also consider their own values and decisions. We can identify the author and illustrator as we read, to emphasize that the book was a creation of real people. Youngsters often develop favorite authors and can search out their books. Even children just a few months old are stimulated and comforted by the sounds and rhythms of an adult reading poems, rhymes, and short stories written for children.

From a baby's viewpoint, anything visible can be enriching. Research has indicated that the contrast between black and white is the most exciting in the early months. Items with a variety of bright colors, textures, sounds, and movements encourage awareness of surroundings. As they become more responsive, children need toys that promote interaction. A good toy gives a child a range of possibilities and encourages initiative. Open-ended toys inspire engagement. A set of blocks can be a fort, a forest, or a sculpture. It is preferable to a wind-up car that travels around in circles. *The test of a good toy is how well it stimulates the child's involvement.* When the child is in charge of the toy, rather than the reverse, he is also in charge of his own play. A good toy is a "catalyst, a means rather than an end."[17]

The best resource of all is a "responsive and available parent."

As specific talents or interests begin to surface, we can provide appropriate materials. For example, chess or checkers, origami paper, blocks, collage materials, scraps of wood, Legos, and computer graphics programs are all stimulating for a child with *spatial ability.* He can enjoy working with and visualizing items in three-dimensional space. An *analytical/mathematical* child thrives on such problem-solving games as Clue, hands-on science activities such as water experiments (with funnels and measuring cups), dominoes, colored counting blocks, toothpicks, graph paper, an allowance and record-keeping notebook, math puzzles, cookbooks, measuring tools, and collections to sort and categorize. Arlene and Roddy, at four, emptied the kitchen cabinet to build towers of canned goods and pots and pans whenever they got together. When we look around our own homes, we discover that almost any ordinary household item can be a learning tool.

Children who *enjoy language* love to make up stories and rhymes, create plays and newsletters, keep journals, play word games, read, and listen to books on tape. Tape recorders, typewriters, and word processors are wonderful tools for such children.

From tapping spoons on glasses to strumming electric guitars, *musical* children have much to enjoy. Youngsters can use wooden sticks, toy xylophones, oatmeal containers (for homemade drums), or hand-held bells for beginning rhythm experiences. When we sing with them, play a musical instrument, or provide audiotapes, they get a feeling for the form of music. Some might want to make up their own songs and perform them. If a tape recorder is available, it can be an asset. For children, hearing themselves on tape is a real treat. Lessons require standard instruments (either rented or bought). Children are most excited with instruments they have chosen themselves. A child who wants to learn to play the French horn should not be forced to take piano lessons. Ensemble playing reinforces a child's skills and enthusiasm. Recitals, school concerts, and local musical performances offer opportunities to appreciate live music. Courses in music theory help children as they advance to understand the structure of what they play. Sometimes children are interested in composing pieces for their own or other instruments. A local music school or university music department can be a good referral source for teachers or courses.

Sometimes we are not comfortable offering an activity our child would enjoy. We all have limits.

Sandy: *When I answered the telephone early one evening, Andrew's teacher was on the line. "Today we had an art project in kindergarten," she began, "and Andrew was uncomfortable and confused with the medium we used. I wonder if he has some allergy we need to know about."*

I reached for the nearest chair, searching my mind; he had no allergies that I knew of. "What were you working with?" I asked in surprise.

> "**M**y mom is here. She loves me very much; she picks me up and takes me to rehearsal."
>
> —Child overheard at a recreation center

"Well, we had rolls of glossy paper and then, of course, regular finger paints."

Uh-oh. I was forced to confess. After sixteen years of child rearing, I could not bear the idea of any more finger painting in my kitchen. Poor Andrew did not know what finger painting was! Fortunately, his school came to the rescue, and he became a happy participant. His work decorated our kitchen for several years.

Resources that are flexible and open-ended in their use inspire our children to explore their talents. Our appreciation for their originality, curiosity, and intensity gives them the feedback they crave. The best resource of all is a "responsive and available parent."[18]

6. Someone to Share Their Enthusiasms

ALTHOUGH THEY ARE an important source of support, parents do not always share a child's interests. Often we have to look elsewhere. Friends, classmates, clubs, community groups, and family members can often provide companionship for a shared interest. Boy Scouts, Girl Scouts, 4-H Clubs, and other such programs provide common goals. Sometimes a camp setting enables a child to find others with his special interests.

Sandy: *Jonathan spent hours alone each day composing music. When we found a camp just for young composers, he made friends as committed to composing as he. He looked forward to renewing those special friendships each summer.*

Brenda loved to paint. She painted flowers, people, scenery, anything she saw. As she progressed, she tried to tackle new challenges—issues of light and shadow, perspective, use of line. Art was important to her, and she was trying to develop her skills. Her mother made a call. Yes, she could bring Brenda over once a week for art lessons. The artist who became her teacher was Brenda's grandmother.

In high school, Chip wanted to try fencing. Unfortunately, no one around him shared that interest. His parents

helped him register for a recreation department class. The teacher recommended a fencing club. There, people of all ages participated. Chip became an enthusiastic fencer and went on to join several fencing organizations.

Adults, both inside and outside the family, can share a child's involvement. They are mentors in their own ways. Sometimes an expert is available; other times just enthusiasm will suffice.

Glen's dad was a fisherman. He lived for the weekends when he could leave his art supply store and take his small boat out on the bay. When Glen was old enough, his dad took him along. Now an adult, Glen has a house with his own little dock and enjoys taking his own children fishing.

Jack was always fascinated with fish and other sea life. He learned about freshwater fishing from books and began to accumulate a collection of hooks, lures, and lines. He haunted fishing supply stores and began to make intricate lures. His father felt guilty about not sharing his son's hobby and decided to take him on a fishing trip. Although it turned out that Jack's dad hooked his son's jacket on one cast and nearly flooded the boat, they both came home happy to have spent the day together.

Sometimes an adult in the community who shares a child's enthusiasm develops a special interest in the child as well. Lois showed an early aptitude for science. She especially loved reading about and collecting rocks and minerals. Needing support beyond school, she worked with a retired geology professor on Friday afternoons. Their friendship continued long past the mentoring experience.

While grandparents can share or encourage a child's interests, they can also provide interesting and unusual information. They can offer a perspective on history. Carl was born in upstate New York in 1910. When he was young, he spent a lot of time in his grandfather's carriage shop. While working, his grandfather told him stories of his experiences as a Union soldier in the Civil War. As a legacy from those shared times, the history of the Civil War became Carl's life-long hobby.

Members of our families and communities are often wonderful resources for our children. Whether the subject is automobile engines or crocheting, young people crave someone to share what they enjoy.

7. Opportunities for Success and Failure

ALTHOUGH WE WOULD like our children to feel successful in their undertakings, disappointment inevitably occurs. An enriched child learns how to deal with failure. When they handle their own problems, children learn to solve them. Parents who allow natural consequences to be the teachers demonstrate trust that their children learn

"Unless we allow them to fail, sometimes grandiosely fail, we cannot allow our children to choose success."

from experience. If Alice does not hang up her wet swimsuit and towel to dry after practice, she will be a cold, wet swimmer when the next day's session begins.

Young children can make mistakes with minor consequences, but older ones are faced with heavier burdens. If we let them fail and try again when they are young, they will cope better with setbacks as they grow. We can teach them to accept mistakes, "capitalize upon them, and learn from them."[19] Because children are inexperienced in decision making, they sometimes make poor choices.

Facing an upcoming piano performance, Sylvia put in a minimal amount of practice time. When she sat down to perform, she stumbled over the music; on her second try, she realized she could not play the piece acceptably. With great embarrassment, she announced to the audience that she could not continue. Natural consequences, her parents felt, would be Sylvia's best teacher. Sure enough, she scheduled regular and more lengthy practice times for herself. The next time she entered a piano competition, she won. "*Unless we allow them to fail, sometimes grandiosely fail, we cannot allow our children to choose success.*"[20]

Children who are not afraid to fail are not afraid to try. Often the learning process is more important than the end result. When we can tolerate our anxieties about our children's imperfections, we give them room to grow. *For children to feel free to develop their talents, they must have the courage to fail and to try again.*

TIPS TO TRY

A. Time

As a family, try to share:
   a meal time, projects, outings, community involvement, and your child's special events.

Individually, children need a parent's presence at:
   bedtime, homework time, and practice time.

B. Stimulating Environment

Visual interest can come through:
   posters, collections, souvenirs, and children's artwork.

For musical variety, try:
   tape recorder, radio, and homemade (or borrowed or rented) musical instruments.

Enhance language with:
   conversation, reading materials, storytelling, and photo albums.

C. Time and Space to Explore

Allow private time in a safe space (child's room, the backyard).

Find a spot (no matter how small) for a child's collections and clutter.

D. Experiences to Expand Interests

Share what you enjoy most with your child:
   hiking, gardening, reading, theater, music, religious faith, and travel.

E. Physical Resources

Children need:
   safe play space, containers for collections, some supplies for arts and crafts, reading and writing materials, and things to sort and categorize (buttons, rocks, and fabric and wood scraps).

F. Someone to Share Enthusiasms

Children need:
   special interest groups of peers (camps, clubs, or classes) and caring adults (family members, neighbors, caregivers, or teachers).

G. Opportunities for Success and Failure

Children need:
   experiences appropriate for their age and ability.

Parents need:
   to read about child development, talk with teachers, talk with other parents, and know their child.
   to allow children to fail and try again.

5

Alone Time

NINE-YEAR-OLD Alex stood in the middle of the kitchen floor, his jaw set, his hands on his hips. "I *can't* go to the Science Club," he wailed. "I have a *conflict*." Alex had always been interested in how things worked. He liked to research problems that intrigued him and to find out the answers on his own. A stickler for getting to the heart of an issue, he never took anyone's word for a solution until he could prove it for himself. Without realizing it, he operated by the scientific method. Today, however, his face was grim. He was having a "discussion" with his mother about a children's program run by the local 4-H Club. "Don't you remember? It meets on Saturday mornings, and *that's* when I watch cartoons!"

> When children solve problems using their own resources, they realize that they *have* resources.

As soon as our children become old enough for lessons and activities, they are on their way to being scheduled and rescheduled and even overscheduled. It is easy to overlook a child's need for time. As busy and caring parents, we want our children to learn to make the best use of their time: to complete assignments, practice their instruments, participate in sports, keep their personal space and possessions in order (a *tall* order!), and enjoy as many enrichment opportunities as possible. The one thing we often neglect to give our children is *time* to themselves.

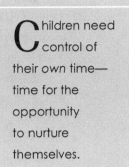

Children need control of their *own* time—time for the opportunity to nurture themselves.

As children grow physically and emotionally, they need personal time to become acquainted with what is going on within themselves: to be in charge of both their bodies and their minds. They need an unstructured private period: time-out—time alone.

With alone time, children enjoy:

1. Relaxation from schedules

2. A release from expectations

3. The power to be in charge

4. Discovering ideas

5. Pursuing projects

6. Dealing independently with problems

7. A sense of identity

8. Meeting age-appropriate needs

9. Creative quiet

Children need control of their *own* time—time for the opportunity to nurture themselves.[1] To busy families, alone time can be a little nerve-wracking. What will Sally *do* if left to her own devices? We worry, of course, about troublemaking behavior, boredom, or aimlessness. In our adult rush to make the most of each moment, we fear that our children's time to themselves is being wasted. Shouldn't he be learning something? What is he *doing?* Shouldn't it be something productive? *The secret all creative people know is that quiet time—time alone—is productive.* As the din of everyday demands is shut out, ideas and inspiration often appear. "Happy people . . . have moments when nothing is on their minds. They welcome these moments, because they open the door for inspiration."[2]

Often lessons and activities become a substitute for parental presence. A child needs private time and space, but within a setting where an adult is available. There is a big difference between *allowing* a child some time alone and *leaving* a child alone regularly. In the case of latchkey children, for example, alone time is not a positive respite; it is a negative constant. Children in these cases need encouragement and some guidance for using their time.

1. Relaxation from Schedules

EVEN VERY YOUNG children have tight schedules. Todd, at five, is frustrated trying to find playtime with his friends. They all have so many activities each week that they rarely have a free day in common. A simple play date has become a complicated logistical accomplishment as well as a special treat. Fourteen-year-old Leslie, intense and cerebral, refuses to wear a watch. Being on time has become a tricky business for her. She often has to ask the time, but she does not mind the inconvenience. She is protesting the need to be on a schedule.

> "Until we teach them differently, children know that life isn't an emergency."

As adults, we think of time like a vessel being filled (sometimes all too quickly). A child sees time very differently. Young children, concerned with how long they have to wait for something to occur, might see time as infinite. But when a youngster is occupied, time does not exist for him. The finger painting, the block building, the insect collecting demand his full concentration. Even calls of "Dinner time!" fail to distract him. He is focused on his pursuits. "*Until we teach them differently, children know that life isn't an emergency.*"[3] They live happily in the present, concentrating on whatever attracts their attention.

Older children see time as a nearly endless commodity to be used at will. For teenagers, deadlines are unsettling, as though someone took away a part of something they owned. When faced with a curfew, their first impulse is to negotiate a later one. Term papers and other events with time limits are especially stressful. As children mature, they attempt to organize their own time around adult demands.

The schedules our *children* keep are the schedules *we* make. When we graft our concept of time onto their lives, we press them into a mold that may be, for them, unnatural. *When they follow our plans, they assume the pressure of following our expectations.*

2. A Release from Expectations

SOMETIMES A CHILD needs a vacation from his own standards.

Linda: *Coming off the soccer field, Aaron moaned, "Today I had a great assist, but I should have been able to score."*

"Oh, no," I reassured my youngest son. "We thought you did great!"

By jumping in with my own judgment and well-meaning support, I gave him less room to explore his own feelings. What he really needed to hear was validation of his reaction ("you sound pretty disappointed"). He had to mull over the game on his own, so he could realistically appraise his strengths and weaknesses.

For every activity, children face expectations—theirs and others'. In *their* time and space, they have the freedom to set their own goals or choose not to. On their own time, choosing *not* to have specific goals must be a permissible option.

Each child must remember that he is not like anyone else; his expectations for himself need to come from within himself. Giving him the opportunity to come to terms with his own limitations is as important as enabling him to recognize his abilities.[4] Only with time alone for introspection can a youngster tap into his own resources. He can do this any place he chooses: his bedroom, the basement, the back steps.

A child can reflect anywhere. He does not need a room full of toys. In fact, the hidden message of material rewards is that the child needs these *things* to be happy.[5] Then the child believes he cannot make *himself* happy. If we let them, children can learn from us that it is okay to "relax and do nothing."[6] We can sit quietly on a park bench; we can take a leisurely walk; we can curl up before a fire. In the peace we provide ourselves, we can entertain new ideas, solve problems, or quietly appreciate our surroundings. We mentor by example.

When a child recognizes that alone time can serve her needs, she can make creative use of it. One young writer used his quiet time for his habit of preserving quotations that were meaningful to him. He preserved them all over the walls and ceiling of his room, the backs of his furniture, and occasionally even in a journal. No one imposed any expectations as to why, where, or how he would make use of this material. This was his way of using his special space and time; he was lucky that his parents respected his privacy in this way. They *did* require him to repaint his room when he left for college.

3. The Power to Be in Charge

CHILDREN NEED SOME autonomy. Alone in her room, twelve-year-old Jenny is a powerful person. With few restrictions, she can structure this environment just the way she wants. If she wants her chair by the window, she can move it there; if she wants to display her collection of hats, she may. The rest of her world spans school, homework, sports, music lessons, dance class, meals, phone calls, and daily chores, all on schedule. In her room, she can loaf, daydream, or work on a project that has no deadline. She is in charge. Her time alone gives her control in a way that the rest of her life does not.

When we hand children some time that is theirs, we are saying that they, too, can have some authority over their lives. They learn that they are, in a very concrete sense, in control of themselves. We also show that we feel they are *capable* of the job. When children grapple with problems, they learn they can resolve them if we allow them the personal time and space to do so. Even babies in their cribs learn to roll over or sit up by being given time to experiment and practice. Success is their reward. Alert parents recognize times when even very young children prefer to be alone; solitary time should be only what is comfortable for the *child*.

Sometimes a child chooses a surprising location to be by himself.

Linda: *When Barry and I took our young sons camping in the summer, we enforced a quiet time rule for an hour every afternoon. Each family member read or played quietly alone, either on his sleeping bag or somewhere nearby. One afternoon during this siesta time, I lazily opened one eye to check on my guys. Seven-year-old Roy had disappeared! I could not see him anywhere. Frantically, I called his name. "Shhh! Mom!" came a soft whisper from overhead. "You're disturbing my quiet time." There sat Roy, a book in his hand, perched on the limb of a tree.*

Alone time can help bolster a talent. For as long as she could re-member, Ruth had loved to draw. Even at age six, she would sit alone on her front porch with a pencil and sketch pad. The world around her came to life on her paper. Anyone who wanted to find her knew where to look. Developing her skills was her own choice. As a grown-up artist, she looked back on this time as an important period of self-nurturing.[7] When we allow our children the gift of their own time, we help foster their self-esteem.

4. Discovering Ideas

INTUITION, INSIGHT, AND creativity all require incubation time, time spent alone with our thoughts. Adrian was excited; he had been shooting baskets all afternoon and had figured out a way of perfecting his hook shot. On his own time, he chose to put his ideas to work, and he was proud of the results. Jess spent hours in his room designing and building model aircraft. He, too, was pleased with his accomplishments. One study showed that a predictor of adult scientific achievement was found to be time in childhood spent alone.[8]

Time alone might yield unexpected results. One little boy liked to spend his time gazing out his bedroom window and lounging in the barn with his family's animals. One day, he watched the hens sitting on their nests and observed their chicks hatching. He returned home embarrassed, his pants seat sticky with egg. He had reasoned that if hens sitting on chicken eggs made them hatch, he would have a try with the goose eggs. His older sister consoled him: "'If no one ever tried anything, even what some folks say is impossible, no one would ever learn anything. *So you just keep on trying . . . and maybe some-day you'll try something that will work.'*" Her younger brother, Thomas Edison, took her advice.[9]

Though our goal might not be to raise great scientists, it *is* to raise competent, fulfilled human beings. When children have time to focus on their own ideas, they can discover that they are capable of *having* ideas to be excited about. When children solve problems using their own resources, they realize they *have* resources.

5. Pursuing Projects

IN HER SELF-CONSTRUCTED setting, a child has no one else to please and can work toward the goals she creates. Jeremy, at sixteen, spends his free time at the piano. He is immersed in composition and always has a work in progress. In a busy home, he tunes out the commotion around him and is alone with his music. The resulting satisfaction, or frustration, is his alone. His parents' support of this time apart implies that they, too, see its value.

Creativity demands time for analysis, exploration, imagination, and evaluation.[10] The family's basement was Shelby's domain. There he spent hours sorting and classifying his extensive rock collection. Interested in the scientific names for his specimens, Shelby carefully researched each one, inserted it in a special plastic box, and labeled it painstakingly. When he was working, he was not to be disturbed. His family respected his wishes.

We have both learned that it is easy to misjudge our children's use of their time.

Sandy: *One afternoon when Andrew was closeted in his room, I knocked on the door and asked what he was doing in there.*

"Just listening to music," came the muffled reply.

"Listening to music?" I was nearly beside myself. The trash needed to be taken out, the school backpack was still on the kitchen floor, and his lizard had no crickets to eat. Later that evening when I heard him talking with a friend about the music on his tapes, I realized my mistake. He was entitled to use a portion of his free time in a way he considered worthwhile.

With their private time, children have the opportunity to do what they like. Olivia spent her free time in her room with music playing. She was choreographing her own dances from musical productions she envisioned in her imagination. In her alone time, she was choreographer, dancer, and producer. Her project was hers alone. When she had completed a routine, she enjoyed teaching it to any interested children she could round up.

6. Dealing Independently with Problems

ALONE TIME CAN help a child recognize that he has the tools to solve his own problems. Six-year-old Nick's block tower kept falling over. Each time he rebuilt it, it toppled again. He began to pound the floor in frustration, but his parents and older brothers wisely did not intervene. Left alone, he eventually redesigned his structure successfully. He was

Sandy: Twelve-year-old Andrew had been spending a lot of time in his room. Every afternoon for a week, he closed the door and shut out the rest of the world. One evening, he emerged very excited. "I've been reading all of the screenplays I collected," he explained. "So now I'm ready to write my own!" Are there any agents out there?

> "One of the most important things you give your child is the gift of independence."
>
> —Trish Magee,
> *Raising a Happy, Confident, Successful Child: 52 Lessons to Help Parents Grow* (Holbrook, MA: Adams Media, 1998), p. 99

proud of the resulting accomplishment. By maintaining their distance, his family expressed confidence in Nick's ability to manage his problems on his own.

Whether our children say, "Do it by self!" as one toddler constantly proclaimed, or request assistance with challenges, *all* children deserve the opportunity to address their own difficulties.

Sandy: Growing up, I loved to draw people. Fashion models were my favorite subjects; I collected magazines and photographs and tried to reproduce them in my sketch book. When I ran into trouble (noses were particularly difficult), I immediately sought help from my mother. A professional artist, she gave me pointers on how to sharpen my visual awareness, while gently encouraging me to solve problems on my own. In spite of our contrasting approaches, both Nick, with his blocks, and I, with my sketch book, were able to benefit from our individual resources.

7. A Sense of Identity

"CHILDREN NEED LOTS of free, quiet time to get used to all that's developing within them."[11] The ever-present closed doors of teenagers' bedrooms remind us of how important separate identities are. From the time children are young, they learn little by little that they are not physically part of their parents. Time by themselves enables them to explore their thoughts and wishes. From the ten-year-old's excited invention of a board game to the fourteen-year-old's locked journal entries, youngsters can find autonomy in their private time.

Even a very young child can choose her own activity within a safe environment. When eighteen-month-old Julie awoke from her nap, she liked to line up all her stuffed animals and talk to them. By selecting her own toys and play, she was asserting her independence. More valuable than a toddler's constant "No!", some time spent alone can remind her, in a positive way, that she is getting bigger and learning to make some decisions for herself. She can make her own choices and be comfortable with her ability to make them.

By being alone, children are reminded that they are individuals. The physical privacy of their personal space reinforces their separateness from everyone else. In turn, they recognize that they have value just for being themselves.

8. Meeting Age-Appropriate Needs

CHILDREN USE TIME alone differently at different ages. Older children can easily daydream or fantasize without tangible stimulation; younger children are more easily drawn to physical objects. They use their time experimenting with choices, discovering cause and effect, engaging in imaginative play, and exploring their own physical capacities. Parents need to make sure play space is safe. Adults can provide a selection of toys that will be intriguing but not overwhelming. The best choices are the ones requiring the *child,* not the toy, to do the work. Simple balls, boxes, and rings, for example, provide more sustained interest than a battery-operated robot. Beginning with ten to fifteen minutes for a one-year-old, we can gradually increase a child's time alone, always being aware that when she seeks us out, it is usually an indication that alone time has been satisfied and is now over.

School-age children respond to more intricate building materials, art supplies, props and costumes for dramatic play, simple musical instruments, and even tape recorders and CD players. Alone time can run from fifteen minutes to over an hour, at the child's dis-

cretion. Although the temptation to permit use of video games, television, and movies is great, the purpose of a child's alone time is to allow her to use her own initiative. As children grow older, they rely less on their external environment and more on their internal resources. A teenage boy ventured, "Solitude for me is a state of mind and not . . . influenced solely by physical surroundings."[12] Alone time may be spent as well in a backyard as in an attic. A nine-year-old could begin a bug collection; a twelve-year-old might compose a poem.

Alone time can be constructive. Ten-year-old Chris spent hours designing race cars and poring over automotive magazines. He wanted to learn what made race cars go fast. Emily, at eleven, spent her free time thinking about social issues; the girls in her class were forming clubs, and she was concerned that her best friend was being left out. In private, she mulled over her feelings and worked on her response. Like Chris and Emily, children can work out their concerns and focus on their interests when left to themselves.

Children need both "inside" and "outside" privacy. They need permission to close the doors to their minds as well as the doors to their rooms. They are grateful when a parent understands and appreciates the need for private thoughts as well as private space. Then *children learn that people cannot eavesdrop on their minds.*[13] By not intruding, parents permit their children to learn that their private time is indeed private.

Quiet space is a wonderful part of alone time. When we show by example that it is okay *not* to be doing something, we teach our children to enjoy, rather than struggle with, their quiet moments.[14] Often we confuse doing nothing with boredom. Boredom is caused by overwhelming our minds. Television, computers, lessons, and games seem to be crowding out those important times when our children can commune with their inner selves.[15] When schedules are so hectic that down time is scarce, we might be sending the message that every minute must be filled. When it is not, our children become dependent on external stimulation and say they are "bored." We must teach them, and ourselves, to cherish times of few demands. First, of course, we have to *make* some of that time. *We may find that doing nothing can be the most creative activity of all.*[16] The relaxation and refreshment of having quiet time are gifts we can give ourselves and our children.

For teenagers, privacy is a central issue. Alone time affords them their personal space. Like younger children, they might use creative materials or prefer to daydream, play music, or write. Telephone time is *not* alone time; it is interactive, not solitary. It affords children important practice in social skills, but it cannot substitute for time alone. When we sit down for a quiet reading time, by example we give our teens permission to take time to be with themselves. On the other hand, if a teenager's alone time begins to eclipse other activities, we need to be available to help him find a balance. For the child who seems to be spending too much time alone, we might suggest scheduling that time as only a small part of his day. If we encourage social activity with his friends or special interest clubs or groups, he might find his own balance.

> The seeds of creativity are nurtured in solitude.

9. Creative Quiet

IN SO MANY cases, the contributions of great individuals came out of their time alone. Henry David Thoreau went to extremes to provide himself with the solitude that he needed. For Virginia Woolf, an afternoon alone became a treasure,[17] and Admiral Byrd found harmony in the silence of Antarctica.[18] A study involving successful sculptors indicated that their most significant form of support was simply to be left alone.[19]

As parents, we can free our children to discover their uniqueness. Time alone forces them to look inward to get to know themselves.[20] They might be surprised by what they find. The insights that emerge from the quiet tend to encourage them in further self-exploration. Though her products may be delightful, a child's ability to tap into her creative process is its own reward. Attentive to her own thoughts and feelings, she can give herself the pleasure of having no prior expectations.[21] Her results need to please only herself. Our children, once accustomed to inner direction, can acquire the pride, pleasure, and confidence so important in the growth of an innovative spirit.[22] The seeds of creativity are nurtured in solitude.

How and when children use their alone time should be their choice. They may use it for emotional needs, cognitive pursuits, or physical activities. They may deal with anger, frustration, or sadness. Children can sort through their own experiences, engage in problem solving, or indulge their creative imaginations. They can perform physical tasks from such project-oriented endeavors as block building, to activities that release pent-up energy, as in playing loud music. *The most important outcome of a child's alone time is not the product; it is the process he has evolved in solitude.* He has learned that he can count on himself and that he is capable of resolving some of his own challenges.

TIPS TO TRY

A. Relaxation from Schedules
Plan for free time each day.

B. Release from Expectations
Model some goal-free use of time:
take a walk, read a book, or listen to music.

C. Power to Be in Charge
Allow a child freedom to choose his own way to spend his personal time.

D. Discovering Ideas
Allow daydreaming; it has its own value.

E. Pursuing Projects
Permitting solitary time allows for creativity.

F. Independence to Deal with Problems
Be patient.
Whenever possible, allow a child to work things out for himself.

G. An Individualized Sense of Identity
Respect children's privacy.
Time alone helps children value themselves.

H. Meeting Age-Appropriate Needs
Alone time needs to be different for different ages.
Don't rush to remove a happy child from a crib;
let her play a while.
With an adult at home:
a few minutes to play alone might be adequate for a very young child; half an hour to himself could be appropriate for an elementary schooler.

I. Creative Quiet
Some of the most innovative ideas and projects can come from quiet time.

6

How Much Is Too Much?

M USIC WAS ALWAYS important in Bryce's family, but Bryce was *not* interested in music. He *was* interested in designing and building cars. From plastic models in his bedroom to larger wood and metal constructions in his garage, he was consumed with his projects. If gears or wheels were available, Bryce could put them to use. As he got older, even the family car was not exempt from his attentions. His parents permitted him to continue to explore what he loved. He grew up to be a professional race car driver. His mother was a concert pianist.

Parents encourage children to develop their interests, and it is appropriate that we should. Although we are concerned about raising anxious children, we also worry about providing them the support they need to succeed in later competitive environments.[1] But how much is too much? When our support becomes coercion, it is too much for our children to handle. When the opportunities we offer become requirements, it is too much. When a child overloads his schedule with more activities than he can comfortably manage, it is too much. To evaluate what *is* appropriate to offer our children, when, and in what way, we need to consider:

1. Lessons

2. Stages of readiness

3. Finding a teacher

4. Practice

5. Encouragement

6. Pushing

Athletic competition can arouse strong feelings about achievement. When young Kerri Strug did her prize-winning gymnastics routine on a sprained ankle to win an Olympic gold medal for her team, audiences were overwhelmed. In the aftermath, many parents asked themselves whether hers was the mind-set that they wanted to instill in their children. Or was she, instead, an example of a young person who had been pushed too hard?

1. Lessons

THERE IS AN adage that all that is necessary for learning is a teacher at one end of a log and a student at the other. The student, however, must be *ready* to learn. If we educate ourselves about children's developmental patterns and are aware of each child's individual attributes, we can recognize when our children are prepared. We can offer support in the form of an enriched home environment and, when appropriate, lessons, summer or after-school programs, or outside mentoring. Most important is our awareness of the difference between encouragement and pushing.

> "Trying to teach young children a structured set of facts about . . . any . . . topic, is a good way to shut off interest valves."

"Childhood should be a journey . . . not a race."

—Bumper sticker

Although a child shows an interest or even an ability in a given area, it is not necessarily time for lessons. Some children do not want outside instruction because they are content working on their own. Perhaps they feel their skills are their private, personal world and prefer to keep it that way. As with Bryce's models and automobile parts, parents can provide a stimulating environment.

Supplies for beginners can be modest. The needs of very young athletes can be served by a collection of balls, sticks, and plastic trash cans or laundry baskets. Budding musicians perform happily on pan lids, sticks, xylophones, coffee cans, and homemade instruments. Michael, an inventive seven-year-old, spent a long period in his room with a shoe box and a large assortment of rubber bands. When he emerged, he happily performed on his new "guitar." Some children prefer a tool bench with simple tools, while others enjoy tinkering with broken clocks or radios. Providing such a resource-rich environment reinforces a child's desire to explore new territory and acquire new skills. We tell him in a concrete way that his efforts are considered worthwhile by his most important adults—his parents.

Children need freedom to experiment before they are ready for the structure of lessons. Natasha's mother was excited. Her quiet, studious five-year-old was intrigued by the sounds of her family's piano. Her mother eagerly enrolled her in formal lessons, and she laboriously learned to produce a melody at the keys. But soon she was no longer interested in the piano and did not attempt another instrument. Fifteen years later, the family's piano is still silent. As a child grows, she might become more interested in formal lessons.

When the developing brain is able to refine input from several senses, at about age seven, a child becomes ready to work with more concrete instruction.[2]

Indeed, a common issue is when to start music lessons. The child who plunks out a tune on the piano or who is enthralled by the organ music at church might not be ready for lessons. In fact, providing lessons at that point could impose an unwanted adult ambition on her child-centered pleasure. "Trying to teach young children a structured set of facts about . . . any . . . topic, is a good way to shut off interest valves."[3] Many children are naturally attracted to music. They eagerly sing, dance, or invent their own melodies. Children can profit from musical experiences prior to developmental readiness for lessons; they should be encouraged to explore. When children are ready to read music, they are able to integrate visual, auditory, and motor patterns, which most cannot do until school age. In fact, for the majority of children, learning to read music should wait until they are quite comfortable reading their own language.[4]

2. Stages of Readiness

WHEN FACING A task that is difficult but within their abilities, children can summon the resources to accomplish something they will be proud of. Eleven girls, all fourth graders, huddled together in a corner of the corral. The girls had all voted enthusiastically to learn horsemanship for their equestrian badges in Girl Scouts. But the horses were huge, the stable was smelly, and none of the girls had ever ridden before. The whole idea was beginning to look like an enormous mistake.

The first lesson concentrated on two things: mounting and dismounting. Some of the girls needed a stool just to reach the stirrups. After their second day of riding, they were all very sore, and on the third day, Betty fell off her horse. By the fifth lesson, the girls could guide their mounts happily around the ring, and even Betty gave her horse a fond pat on its flanks as she dismounted. After the tenth lesson, each of the girls stepped forward proudly to receive her equestrian badge. They now had new respect for the extras in Western movies and new respect for themselves as well.

Research indicates that children experience different stages in their readiness. First, youngsters are content with what comes freely.[5] Then they might ask for help. From about ages seven to ten, children concentrate on specifics. Rules and practical ideas have new appeal. Beginning lessons in these years of middle childhood provides the comfort of stated limits and concrete tasks.[6] Kids at this age, like the horseback riders, need to learn patience to achieve the results they anticipate. From the security of this background, teenagers can consciously work to develop mastery. Adolescents are independently able to plan, put into effect, and evaluate projects; creative young people try new things and are willing to take risks.[7]

Readiness for lessons also assumes readiness to practice. The preschooler, whose attention span is limited, is not ready for the restrictions practice entails. Entering middle childhood, however, children can focus on specific tasks for longer periods. They are able to be responsible for themselves in many areas, including the discipline of practice; they can follow a routine. In a study of exceptionally talented individuals, researchers found that motivation and effort are more significant than a child's particular gifts or special qualities.[8] A child who studies a musical instrument or undertakes a new physical skill, for example, needs to understand that a new skill takes an investment of time and effort. He needs encouragement to be patient with both. "A child gradually realizes that talent comes through habits of hard work."[9]

In seeking to provide resources and learning opportunities, parents face several options: group lessons, specialized summer programs, residential programs, private lessons, consultations, and outside mentoring. The age, area of interest, and personal characteristics of each child influence a family's choice.

> A child gradually realizes that talent comes through habits of hard work."

Group lessons can be stimulating, enabling children to meet others with the same interests. In group settings, children often find themselves learning from each other, as well as from the instructor, but the size of the group is important. An art class, for example, should be no larger than ten students per teacher.[10] Any small group maximizes the amount of interaction among students and between student and teacher.

Specialized summer and residential programs offer group instruction in different kinds of settings. Camps, college campuses, science laboratories, national parks, and zoos provide stimulating environments. At seventeen, A.J.'s interest in animals drew him to a university summer zoo program. Amber, at eleven a dedicated ballet student, studied dance weekly with her city ballet company. A budding naturalist, ten-year-old Jane enjoyed a junior rangers program in a national park. Residential music programs can be attractive to older students serious in their musical studies. Matt, interested in oceanography, spent three weeks away from home in a marine science program for high school students. Surrounded by peers devoted to her interests, a child with a special talent can feel that she is a part of a group instead of feeling different.

Private lessons have the advantage of providing strong student-teacher interaction while maintaining flexibility to progress at the child's pace. Greg liked math. At a young age, he tried to figure out difficult equations and concepts. His parents decided private lessons might provide the stimulation of someone to work with. The sessions helped Greg concentrate on his desired skill and interests, and he became confident and competent. Sometimes even when a child pursues a group activity, such as school band, private lessons will help him further sharpen his skills.

Consultations are appropriate when a child does not want private or group lessons, but would like some help once in a while.[11] An adolescent's independent work, such as a science project, might lend itself to this kind of arrangement. *A mentor* brings a more individualized and intense focus to his interaction with a child.

3. Finding a Teacher

WHATEVER THE FORMAT, effective teaching includes three basics. In evaluating a teacher, parents should look for the following qualities:

Strong Communication Skills. A teacher must be able to suit his material and his presentation to the level and maturity of his student. "I can't ask my teacher about it," seven-year-old Katherine complained to her mother. "I never understand his explanations!" Is the teacher comfortable with beginners? Can the teacher communicate a clear picture of his goals for the student? Is he willing to work *with* the student to develop those goals? Does he treat children respectfully rather than patronizingly?

A Supportive Attitude. When giving a lesson, does the teacher allow interruptions from telephone, doorbells, or visitors? Does she maintain a consistent lesson schedule? Does she acknowledge her students' efforts, even when the results are not stellar? Is she receptive to her students' preferences for specific material? Enthusiasm and concern for her students are characteristic of a supportive teacher.

The teacher who arranged for fifteen-year-old Anna to take her final exam in an empty office understood her student's need to concentrate in a low-stress environment. Mrs. Gordon, who sent Justin notes urging him to submit his writing to the school newspaper, let this student know she appreciated his work.

Knowledge of the Subject Matter. Because the teacher's purpose is to share knowledge or skills, parents seek a teacher highly competent in his field. Does he specialize in only one level of student? What is the teacher's current connection with his field? A retired professor might continue to read journals in his subject area; a music teacher might play in a community orchestra.

So how do we find such a teacher? Word-of-mouth referrals are often reliable. A more knowledgeable friend or professional could have suggestions. A gifted student might recommend his teacher. Behind each talented student, there is usually an excellent teacher.[12] An instructor whose students enjoy their time with him sounds promising. Children can ask their friends. When we make an appointment to meet a teacher, we are not making a hiring commitment. Regardless of his renown, a teacher must fit the needs of our *child,* rather than the child having to adapt to this teacher's style.

An introductory session between teacher and student can be helpful. We and our child should come to the meeting prepared with questions. They can be as specific as our individual needs (scheduling, practice hours) or as general as those discussed earlier. Our interactions with the teacher should feel comfortable. As parents, we can sit in on a young child's meeting and evaluate what we hear; we need to rely on an older child's reaction and preference, because he probably will not want us to sit in. (Scheduling and other details can be clarified on the phone.) Sometimes parents or students can visit a prospective teacher's class to assess his effectiveness. Our child needs to know that the student-teacher relationship belongs to him and his teacher and can be open to reevaluation and change as needed.

An *outside mentor* is a unique kind of teacher. In addition to serving as a tutor in a specific area, a mentor can become an instructor in life.[13] It is helpful for a child of any age to have an adult, in addition to her parents, who is particularly interested in her. A common bond such as an interest  or talent might draw student and mentor to each other; mutual respect and caring keeps them together.

Though his mentor was a professional artist, Derek Walcott was encouraged to follow his creative passion, and he became a successful playwright.[14] As in Walcott's case, a mentor's field could be different from his student's. The significance is in his involvement and support. A mentor needs to provide feedback appropriate to the student's age and skill level. He also enables the child to practice interacting with another person.

Sandy: *At ten, Stephen and his mentor, a retired chemistry professor, used to have long arguments about almost any subject. They began by working on chemistry, but they discovered mutual interests in politics, history, and literature. Because Stephen recognized that the professor knew more than he (at least about chemistry!), he listened attentively.*

The difference between a mentor and a teacher is often one of intensity. The ratio of mentor to student is one to one, and the commitment is usually of the same level. Like the child's parent, an outside mentor invests in her student's progress and derives genuine pleasure from his successes. She is able to view her student as a developing *person*, not only as a developing talent.

Sandy: When Daniel applied to college, he included a lengthy musical composition he had been working on for most of the school year. Unfortunately, it was still unfinished. His mentor, a musician and composer himself, reassured him that it was worthy of consideration and that he could mark it a "work in progress." (Someone at the college must have agreed with his mentor; Daniel was accepted.)

In a sense, we are all works in progress. A mentor recognizes this and employs the patience of someone who realizes that he is panning for gold in a very rich vein; eventually he will be successful. Responding to such support, our child can explore his field, stretch his talents, and absorb some of the confidence directed his way. Failure is a part of learning; successful people remember how long it took to achieve their goals.

4. Practice

WHEN CHILDREN ARE ready to learn, they must be ready to practice. And an adult should be ready to *be there*. No matter how brief, our presence shows we care. It is hard to work on a developing skill when no one is around to acknowledge the effort. A family can appreciate its members in a way no one else can. Whether it is in the living room or at the playing field, our being there is very powerful support. It not only teaches our children that we care; it also models supportive behavior for each member of the family. We would like each child to grow up to value his family members as we value him.

Albert, at ten, is very serious about his cello playing. His mom is at work all day, so he practices during dinner preparation time, keeping her company in the kitchen. Even amid the clanging and banging of pots and pans, he is aware that she is listening. When he is especially proud of his work, he will also seek out his brother to hear him play.

FIVE WAYS TO HELP A CHILD PRACTICE

1. Be there.
2. Arrange a daily practice time.
3. Agree on length of practice.
4. Be familiar with practice content and goals.
5. Be encouraging.

With our child, we can develop a practice schedule we expect her to meet. She can make a chart as a visual reminder. She can keep a calendar or have her own colored marker to keep track on the family calendar. Colorful stickers, stars, or check marks can serve as reinforcements or rewards when practice is complete. When a child is involved in her own scheduling, she is more likely to follow it.

A teacher or coach can suggest an appropriate practice time frame. Because it will have the sanction of his instructor, a child will be more likely to respect it. A clock or timer will give him a concrete sense of the time to be covered.

If the teacher or coach clarifies what is expected from each practice, a child knows how his practice period should be divided. How or when to include skill building, new material, and review are important components of each practice. When we ask our child (before he begins) what his goals are for that practice session, he can then focus on the time as a work session, not an exercise in drudgery.

We can offer encouragement rather than praise: "All your work really shows" or "That scale was tricky." Our support acknowledges our child's attempt. Praise reflects judgment. It evaluates his product according to *our* standards, not his. Criticism is out of place here. Logical consequences usually result from both hard work or no work; a teacher or coach can easily pick up on problems. Our job is to assist in the week's effort and the next set of goals. Our appreciation for the subject is important; remember, our child chose it.

5. Encouragement

SELF-CONFIDENCE IS THE result of encouragement (the root word is *courage*). Parents who appreciate a child's *effort* instead of his ability[15] are giving their child the tools to achieve. In Benjamin Bloom's study of exceptionally high-achieving adults, the parents had been regularly available to help with their children's problems and to support efforts and accomplishments.[16] Parental support comes in different forms. When we set aside even a small amount of time to focus on each child daily, we show genuine interest in what our child is working on. We are paying attention to what is important to him. Even when success does not follow effort, *parents should recognize the courage of trying.* A child who never risks cannot grow. We need to be as ready with empathy in disappointment as with applause for triumph. No matter how old we are, we can still remember those moments when our efforts were appreciated.

> A child who never risks cannot grow.

Linda: Aaron, seventeen, and his friend, Jana, were reminiscing about their performances in their elementary school talent show. Now a high school actor and a student government leader, they remembered their joy in these early accomplishments. Dressed in a brown garbage bag, her rendition of a singing raisin ("Heard It Through the Grapevine") and his monologue of "Why Every Boy Needs a Box" were, in their minds, the hits of the evening. The parents and teachers who put together the yearly programs made certain that every child who wanted to be involved had a part. The adults emphasized participation rather than result.

"The only time you fail is when you fail to try."

—Diane Ippolito,
assistant superintendent, Albemarle County, VA, schools,
interview with authors, June 30, 1998

Praise and encouragement are different. Praise imposes someone else's values. Encouragement will acknowledge the effort, leaving appraisal to the artist. Nine-year-old Ethan had just completed a project. He was working on a sort of family crest with different pictures for different family members' interests. Not paying attention, his father said, "That's great." Ethan responded, "No, it's not," and proceeded with a catalogue of his mistakes. What Ethan wanted to hear was encouragement, not praise. "I'm glad you're working on such an interesting project" or "What a lot of effort you're putting into your work" would have been more supportive and, in Ethan's view, more realistic. Encouragement builds process and improvement. With praise, the focus is on the product.[17] Children who work for praise try to please someone other than themselves. Their rewards are *external* and require greater and greater visibility. The father who gives money for a good report card, the mother who bribes a child with ice cream for each practice period, the grandmother who sends a gift for every game won all make the child's success *theirs*, not the child's. The *internal* rewards that come with a child's effort

Children need to know they are "loved because of who they are."

—Chris Wallace,
ABC News correspondent, interview with authors, June 11, 1998

need no embellishment. Through encouragement, parents convey belief in a child's capabilities.

In addition to results (the third-place ribbon at the swim meet, the honorable mention certificate at the science fair), children need support at other times. When they are struggling with a difficult task or just tackling a project on their own, we affirm our faith in their abilities through encouragement. Children are especially vulnerable when:

they have problems

they go through important life changes (school, family, developmental)

their efforts are not meeting with success

they are late bloomers

they are coping with learning disabilities[18]

A smile, a hug, a pat on the shoulder, or just time taken to listen can show our awareness of something positive in a child. Sensing our respect for his efforts, a child is motivated to continue. Sixteen-year-old Daryl, who rarely performed for the rest of his family, continued to play his violin when-

ever his mom stayed in the room. Although he did not want to discuss his work, his mother's presence and interest were evidence of her support. Alison put much effort into redecorating her bedroom. She hung new pictures on the walls and rearranged all of her knick-knacks on her shelves. Exhausted but smiling, she bounded downstairs to report to her parents, "It was a lot of work, but my room really looks great! Come see!" Whether our children absorb support as part of their environment, like Daryl, or actively seek it, like Alison, they all crave it.

6. Pushing

MORE THAN A'S and awards, a safe, accepting environment enables a child to confront her difficulties. When we promote challenges our children are unprepared to tackle, we are imposing stress. Just as praise itself is a form of pressure, an environment of expectations too high for the child is also unproductive. Thirteen-year-old Joan was running for class vice president. She had to give a speech before the assembled student body prior to the election. "It's the most important speech of my life!" she wailed, pacing around the house. Her father, a man of high standards, sympathized. "Why don't we work on this together?" he suggested. The resulting speech was worthy of a college debate class but unworthy of Joan's young audience. Neither they nor she understood or appreciated what she produced. Her father had written it all himself. He had the sense of accomplishment; his daughter did not.

Lessons begun too young, contests at early skill levels, exacting standards of conformity, acceleration of pace or grade level contribute to pressure on children. Children under stress will be afraid to take chances on trying something new. Research has identified Type A behavior (demanding, competitive) with associated raised cholesterol levels in children. These two conditions are connected with pressure for achievement by parents.[19] Children must be realistic about their goals. The squeaky violin, the unidentifiable clay sculptures, and the constant free-throw practice are activities children delight in. They become adults who enjoy picking out familiar songs on the piano and relish a neighborhood game of softball. When we surrender the belief that an acceptable product should result from every activity, we give children permission to be self-directed.[20]

In their first artistic explorations, children have no preconceptions. Flowers can be any color, shape, or size. If an adult imposes standards such as sanctioned shapes, sizes, and

"Don't impart the notion that your kids always have to be the best. Kids should be what they are."

—D. Anthony Stark,
composer, interview with authors, June 29, 1998

colors, the child learns to disparage his own creativity. The little girl whose first-grade art experiences require the coloring in of printed pictures later might not like to draw at all. Six-year-old Dale was frustrated with his artwork. It did not look like his friends said it was supposed to. One day his mother gave him a book of abstract art and showed him that some famous artists made pictures that did not look realistic. He discovered that an artist had the freedom of creativity, to work to standards that were his alone. Dale took the book to bed with him every night for a month.

Even a child's free time can fall victim to adult standards and pressures. The push for performance in everything she does drains a child of her autonomy. When she feels she has to be the best member of the team, the highest scorer on the math test, the winner of the citizenship award, she is less likely to be able to differentiate the demands of the outside world from her own desires. Summertime, which used to represent freedom and relaxation for children, is now often heavily programmed for them. A new attitude, visible in the focus of many summer camps, is that "the years of childhood are not to be frittered away by engaging in activities merely for fun."[21] The expectation is instead that children will use their time to develop skills in areas that adults deem particularly worthwhile. Tennis has replaced whittling or hopscotch; piano studies have edged out washboard bands.

When we nurture our children's talents, we nurture the seeds of their growth. As with any other ingredients, too much or too little in the way of expectation defeats the purpose. With the right amount, they can flourish.

TIPS TO TRY

A. Lessons
   Recognize:
   a child's readiness, his need to explore, and the value
   of his experiences.
B. Stages of Readiness
   Natural:
   Children are content with their own resources.
   Practical:
   Children are interested in specifics—rules and lessons
   are appropriate.
   Mastery:
   Adolescents are able to plan, put into effect,
   and evaluate projects independently.
C. Finding a Teacher
   Look for:
   strong communication skills, a supportive attitude,
   and knowledge of the subject matter.
   Children can learn from:
   group lessons, private lessons, specialized programs,
   consultation, or mentoring.
D. Practice
   Child must be ready for structure.
   Agree on:
   a practice schedule, time, and content.
   Be there.
E. Encouragement
   Give encouragement (support), not praise (judgment).
F. Pushing
   Avoid:
   lessons begun too young, competition at early skill
   levels, exacting standards of conformity,
   and unnecessary acceleration of pace or grade level.

7

Technicalities

CARDBOARD BOXES AND Styrofoam blocks were everywhere. The Barnes family had just purchased its first computer. Everyone was engaged in setting it up. While Devin, six, and Serge, nine, began assembling the parts and plugging them in, their technologically challenged parents contributed such information as, "Be careful! Don't drop that—it cost a fortune!" and "The electrical outlets are over here." After hours of assembling, loading, and downloading significant software, the magic machine was ready to work. The two boys edged up with their faces nearly flattened against the computer screen, and Mom and Dad decided to let them begin their electronic relationship on their own. Soon whoops of joy echoed through the house. "Come quick!" the boys called, "It works great! We made the computer *moo!*"

Imagine a computer the size of a living room, whose myriad beeps, buzzes, and blips require a staff of white-coated experts to respond. Some of us are old enough to remember that this was not science fiction; that was the way it really was. What a long way we have come in the last forty years. Today laptop computers are almost as common as portable televisions. Toddlers can press buttons and make astonishing things happen. The question is not *whether* our children need to become computer literate, but *when* and *how*. Technological tools are essential. When children use a computer, they make decisions and choices. As one child put it, "'TV . . . does what it wants to do. A computer does what *you* want it to.'"[1]

Growing up with technology all around them, children are much more comfortable with complex electronics than their parents. So if we need help entering the computer age, we do not have far to go; we can just enlist the aid of a child.

> "'TV . . . does what it wants to do. A computer does what you want it to.'"

Sandy: *Luckily for me, I still have one son at home for technical assistance. Recently I needed my thirteen-year-old once again. Desperately pushing keys in an attempt to find an Internet list evaluating new cars, I simply could not figure out how to pull up information on the latest models. Without looking up, Andrew matter-of-factly responded, "I don't know any more than you, Mom. Just fool around a little and you'll get it!"*

Here is the latest generation gap in a nutshell: kids are not afraid to fool around and play with electronic equipment. Some parents, however, fear losing forever whatever is on their screens. It is worth remembering, as we step out into this electronic world, that "a computer takes at least as much planning as raising a new puppy."[2] And at least as much information and assistance. Alongside perhaps more familiar marvels of technology, computers are yet another element of our multimedia environment.

What should parents know as we approach these blinking, clicking, buzzing, expensive pieces of equipment? Here, for starters, are some basic categories to consider:

1. Computers: what, why, how

2. Electronic games: to play or not to play?

3. Computer programs

4. "'Net"-working

5. Television and its friend, the VCR

6. Multimedia

One of the most pressing concerns parents have, besides how and whether to pay for a computer setup, is whether we need to know how to work it. We do not necessarily learn to play the saxophone when our child takes lessons or work out for football when our child is on the team.

> S tudies have found that the presence of an adult during computer use finds children more involved and less frustrated.

Eleven-year-old Rachel was making impressive headway with her computer skills, but she became frustrated. She needed someone who could answer all the questions that arose as she worked. She was significantly ahead of what her teachers and classmates understood, and her parents were completely befuddled by her technological abilities. But they knew how to find help. Through the local high school's math department chairman, Rachel's mother was able to find a computer-savvy high school student. For helping the enthusiastic fifth grader, she was thrilled to earn a weekly fee. They worked together throughout that school year and the following summer, to the great satisfaction of everyone concerned.

To enable our children to access this important resource, we as their mentors do need to have some understanding of what it involves. Whether to become thoroughly computer literate ourselves remains an option, unless, of course, we are already computer users. Studies have found that with the *presence* of an adult during computer use, young children are more involved and less frustrated.[3]

1. Computers: What, Why, How

WHAT *IS A* computer? It is simply a machine that can receive and store information. It follows instructions to manipulate, record, save, and print that information. Why does a child need to use one? It is a learning tool whose user can initiate the learning, making the process more enjoyable, productive, and independent. When a youngster uses computer games, puzzles, and other creative software, she is learning to make comparisons, initiate her own responses to problems, and manipulate symbols. She is engaging in "active learning."[4]

Software and problem-solving programs introduce and expand new subject areas. Word processing fosters writing. Graphics and music programs add interest to projects and inspire creativity. The Internet enables students to communicate with each other and tap into further resources. Learning to program lets students decide what the computer will do and devise commands to make it happen, using a combination of graphics and printed instructions.

Computer technology gives children a special opportunity; they can enter the world of "what if," experimenting as much as they want with their hypotheses.[5] Open-ended in nature, computers enable their users to create: "electronic journals, diaries, stories, notes, signs, maps, games." Users can reread, revise, edit, redesign, and print in different formats; they can "draw, graph, compose music, or play writing-reading games."[6]

It is not only the explosion of information but the skills required to have access to that information that our children need to master. Because information is transmitted via a keyboard, *typing has become an essential skill even for very young children;* they need to learn to type as soon as they can comfortably read and write. As the old card catalogues disappear from libraries and computer screens proliferate, it is clear that every child must become computer literate. Programmed to repeat and reteach the same fact without losing patience, computers respond regularly with positive feedback (adults sometimes forget to). The independence of computer use encourages children to search for information on their own. Particularly exciting is the instantaneous access that computers provide. By keeping pace with the skills of the individual child, computers offer a major advantage.[7]

Is there no disadvantage to this wonderful invention? There is, and it is significant. Like any other learning tool, *a computer is only helpful when it is used appropriately.* When a computer is used as a substitute baby-sitter, it is detrimental to a child. When it replaces friendships and other interpersonal relationships, the consequence can be impaired social development. When it edges out a child's time to experiment with *real* objects and physically explore his world, it hampers his ability to learn.

We now know from research that the neural connectors in the brain are stimulated from information received through *physical manipulation* of objects in a child's environment.[8] Wooden or foam blocks, water, sand, and finger paint are some of the important sensory materials all children need to explore. Later abstractions such as number, volume, weight, and height rely on the concrete experiences children receive. As a *supplemental* tool, a computer permits a child to investigate and create in a world of symbols, the next step up from the world of tangible objects.

Because technology quickly becomes obsolete, some parents wonder whether an investment in both expensive equipment and training to use it is necessary. Why should a youngster learn to operate a system that will soon be outdated? Will he have to unlearn the skills he has just acquired? Never fear; all learning is cumulative. New skills build on the earlier ones; *children learn everything in stages, and technology is no exception.* To them, it is natural to progress from one set of skills to the next. Just as in learning to read, they learn one level only to move forward, always building on what came before. As for the equipment itself, children work creatively with any computer hardware and software; in most cases, what they have available to them will not become obsolete for *their* uses for eight to ten years.[9]

So how should we begin? Many sites offer free or inexpensive computer use. Libraries, copy centers, schools, community centers, and colleges provide up-to-date equipment and flexible hours. Not every home has to have a computer.

Currently, a complete computer system includes:

- the computer

- a keyboard

- a monitor (screen)

- a printer

- a CD-ROM drive

- a sound card

The issue is not just the selection of the computer itself. To *use* the new technology, also needed are:

- a modem (uses a telephone line; be prepared—a second line or some strict rules for usage time might become necessary)

- networking cables

- surge protector (protects computer from power fluctuations)

- electrical outlets (many things plug in!)

If opting for computer ownership, factors to consider in *selection* are:

- ease of use

- longevity (best combination of cutting-edge technology and ability to update)

- performance

- communication capacity (Internet)

- multimedia software (some might come with the computer)

- service and reliability

- comparative value

A good place to start is with a reputable dealer and lots of written materials to review carefully at home. Checking a consumer evaluation journal is also wise.

Unlike a toaster, a computer does not just plug in. We need good resources for setting it up and learning to use it. Here is where our "techie" friends can really perform a service, unless we are able to rely totally on our knowledgeable children. Those who speak "computerese" probably can make initial contact more comfortable. In addition, a reliable dealer can suggest appropriate computer magazines for beginners, tapes and instructions, and information on clubs and user groups.

2. Electronic Games: To Play or Not to Play?

"'**V**ideo games are revolutionary; they are the beginnings of human interaction with artificial intelligence.'"

Sandy: I made the mistake of worrying too much about my boys playing video games. I kept a close watch on computer use and tried to discourage game playing at every opportunity. After an admirable high school career, Jonathan left for college. Welcoming me to his dorm suite on parents' weekend, he proudly pointed out his posters, his new coffee table, and his area rug. But the best he saved for last. "Want to see something really neat?" Grinning from ear to ear, he switched on his new laptop computer and pulled

"The children [who end up becoming] most hooked on video games are those with few interests."

—Joan Anderson and Robin Wilkins.
Getting Unplugged: Take Control of Your Family's Television, Video Game, and Computer Habits (New York: Wiley, 1998), p. 73

up a bright and bleeping video game. "Isn't this great?" he crowed. "Now I can play video games all I want!"

A magnet for children, video games are often troubling to parents. The prevalence of violence, stereotypes, and escapist scenarios can capture a child's attention for prolonged periods. Too much involvement in video fantasy worlds can cause a child to become impatient with the less controllable "real" world. However, the positive effects for children can frequently counterbalance the equation. Just as with television viewing, we need to know what our children are interacting with on-screen.

Linda: *Both of us had the experience of our children—knowing of our disapproval—saving and pooling their money with others to buy video game systems behind our backs! In my case, for a few months, Roy was making surprisingly frequent visits to his friend's house down the street. I was pleased that they were enjoying being together, and, with the parents home, it never occurred to me that I might not like what the kids were doing. Then one evening his friend came to our house, lugging a large box labeled "Nintendo." "Here," he said. "It's Roy's turn to keep our Nintendo for the next three months." If our boundaries are too extreme, kids do find a way around them.*

A gateway to more serious computer use, video games permit interactive response. "'Video games are revolutionary; they are the beginnings of human interaction with artificial intelligence.'"[10] What happens on the monitor results from the player's choices. The first medium to combine dynamic visual displays with a child's active participation, video games capitalize on colorful moving imagery. Like television, the medium of video games is values-neutral. It is game selection and amount of playing time that influence our children's ideas. Violent action, sexual themes, or other inappropriate content are clearly not fit for children. We fear that players learn violent behavior from violent games, but it has been found that *two*-player video games of aggression—cooperative *or* competitive—actually *reduce* children's levels of aggressive play.[11] Perhaps playing with a partner contributes to cooperation and releases aggression, while playing alone may provide no outlet. Cooperatively oriented games stimulate further positive interactions by demonstrating that cooperation is rewarded. Parental responsibility entails knowing and approving (or rejecting) what our children are playing.

Some skills (surprise!) *are* actually enhanced by video game play. Nathan and Brad, ages eight and ten, were literally pulling on their mother's sleeves. "C'mon, Mom, we'll only play a couple of games," they pleaded. A neighborhood shopping mall included among the stores a brightly beckoning video arcade. The haze and bedlam of the game room were clearly not appealing to a thirty-five-year-old woman, so the boys couched their appeals developmentally. "It's good for us, you know," they confided. "It helps improve our eye-hand coordination!" We are not so sure video games would have helped Lou Gehrig or Hank Aaron, but some skills *are* required for playing computerized games.

Electronic games require the ability to respond to simultaneously moving images. Players develop their levels of cognitive complexity as they learn to coordinate visual information coming at them from more than one perspective.[12] Frequently, adults find this task much harder than their children; in this case, our children are the veterans and we are the novices. Time is also a significant factor; the speed of a player's reaction can determine his effectiveness. Flexibility and independence are rewarded in video game play. There are all sorts of obstacles in an electronic game. No one even tells the player the rules; they must be deduced through play, a particularly terrifying thought for parents who rely on the security of rules. Children take charge of the process by issuing commands and instructions and figuring things out for themselves. They take risks, make errors, and correct themselves as they play.[13] Deductive reasoning, strategizing, and thinking are positive hallmarks of electronic game play.

Linda: "Just let him play games," Roy's fourth-grade teacher told me. "He'll learn how to program the computer that way." This teacher wanted us to provide computer time for him, so she generously sent him home from school nearly every Friday with her personal computer for the weekend. He enjoyed experimenting with computer games. Within the next few years, he designed and sold a video game and sold an article to a computer magazine. He had, indeed, learned how to program.

We adults are "paper trained;" many of us have learned to use paper, not data banks and screens for information.[14] In contrast, our children's world is flooded with blinking lights and moving images of the technology they grow up with. However uncomfortable we might be, we do recognize that our children benefit from using a technology that often begins with games. Our responsibility is to make sure that the games they are using and the time spent playing them are appropriate. Kids play electronic games outside their own homes, so keeping in close touch with other parents is essential. For children, parent networks are as important as electronic networks.

3. Computer Programs

TO BE ABLE to create a video game is what motivates children to learn to program a computer. Programming requires the ability to manipulate symbols. A computer program is a set of instructions written in symbols that tells the computer exactly what functions to perform. Software contains packaged computer programs that run on the hardware of the computer. Software offers our children opportunities to "write (word processing), publish (desktop publishing), draw and paint (graphics), store and retrieve information (databases), design (LOGO), compose (music), share writing with others (telecommunications), and have fun with language (learning games)."[15] It is helpful for children to have access to a software library—at home, at school, or in the public library system. *At its best, software is interactive.* Question/answer and drill/practice programs can provide skill reinforcement but cannot teach anything new.

> "Perhaps the most valuable thing we can learn is not how to make . . . the games less addictive, but how to make other learning experiences . . . more so."

In selecting software, we should look at magazine articles and seek user reviews (not the salesperson's enthusiastic pitch). When we buy or borrow programs one at a time, we enable our children to explore and become comfortable with each of them before moving on. We want material that:

- is compatible with the computer's capabilities

- is age-appropriate for our children

- offers open-ended answers

- provides positive feedback

- is not violent in content

- encourages problem-solving, creativity, and thinking skills

The most popular program used by students is word processing, turning the computer into a smart typewriter and an "electronic filing cabinet."[16] Words and sentences can be arranged and rearranged on the screen prior to printing; this flexibility is extremely helpful with children for whom handwriting or rewriting are laborious exercises. A number of programs contain creative options that make writing fun.

Students view their written product on a computer screen; they can change words or whole sections of their work including underlining, spacing, and style and size of lettering. They can automatically check their spelling and search through an electronic dictionary and thesaurus. Children working on projects via computer have been found to improve the quality and creativity of their work and to work together more effectively.[17] Desktop publishing enables students to design pages, storybooks, posters, signs, cards, calendars, and so forth; they can publish school newsletters and lay out yearbooks as well as produce all sorts of creative literary and arts magazines. Among the most exciting uses of a computer are music and graphics programs. Children can compose music and listen to it in progress, and they can see their own computer-generated drawing and painting on-screen.

As exciting as all these computer learning experiences are, we do not want to lose sight of the value of nonelectronic opportunities. Building something from scratch, watching a live performance, or reading an absorbing book can all stimulate children. "Perhaps the most valuable thing we can learn is not how to make . . . the games less addictive, but how to make other learning experiences . . . more so."[18]

4. "'Net"-Working

AS WITH VIDEO games, parents need to keep a watchful eye on youngsters' use of the Internet. Eleven-year-old Angelo, fresh from a month at camp, was devastated; he missed his friends and despaired of ever making contact with them. When his dad reminded him that he might be able to reach some of them on the Internet, his whole face lit up. He began spending many afternoons typing on the computer and one day announced with pride, "Now I have my own *free* e-mail account. Nora, my friend from camp, helped me get it. My new address is KICKASS@hotmail.com!"

E-mail is one of the Internet's most popular features. Requiring no postage, phone calls, or voice messages, it can send and receive messages almost instantaneously and at the convenience of the user. E-mail is a computer system that can send and receive written messages, pictures, sounds, and video images.[19] We can send the same message to multiple addresses simultaneously.

E-mail is not *private;* people using it need to remember that it is a written record and not confidential. We have to caution our children never to share through e-mail any self-identifying details such as real names, addresses, phone numbers, credit card numbers, social security numbers, and passwords. This requires parental permission. If someone unknown to the user requests to verify such information on-line, it is important that we notify our service provider immediately; children need to know this. Chat rooms enable people to converse with each other on-line in real time, almost like talking on the telephone. Our children should proceed with caution; people sometimes lie about where and who they are online. Responses may range from rudeness to actual harassment.[20]

> The most important tool we can use is conversation.

Prevention includes equipping our children with the knowledge to recognize what is objectionable and how to avoid it. The ESC (escape) key and the power switch on the computer enable any child to withdraw quickly from an uncomfortable situation. Though we can put safety controls (in the form of software) on our computers, children still have access to computers outside our homes; also, we may inadvertently block concepts with positive ramifications, such as alcohol and drug education information. But the most important tool we can use is conversation. Talking with our kids about what is objectionable and what to do about it encourages them to be comfortable with their own responses and with their access to us.

It is a good idea to install our computers in a well-trafficked spot in our homes. All the guys came to Ned's house more and more frequently to do homework together. His computer was in a corner of the basement where they could work undisturbed. Only when his mother peeked in unannounced one afternoon did she discover what they were working on. Ned was accessing "dirty pictures" for everyone to share.[21]

Creative names like Angelo's for e-mail accounts are only one source of parental discomfort with the Internet. Our children understand it so much better than we do. The Internet is a worldwide network of computers connected electronically. Through a common language, they can exchange information globally. The World Wide Web is one collection of electronic documents within the Internet. Simple mouse clicks make it possible for the user to move readily from one document to another: "surfing the 'Net." Through a commercial online service or national Internet service provider, we can connect our computers to the Internet. Before selecting a service, we again need to consult our favorite "techies" or local experts.

Even though computers become obsolete in a shorter period of time than, for example, bicycles, they are still valuable tools despite their age. As one computer camp director emphasized, children do not need the most up-to-date equipment to learn computer skills.[22] There are arguments both pro and con about the value of computer use for children under six. Some experts note that the fine-motor activity involved with computers (use of keyboard and mouse) could interfere with time better spent in the important age-appropriate large-motor tasks (climbing, running, jumping, large block play). Others cite research recognizing social and cognitive growth as results of computer activity.

Children using a computer alone for too long a period might be missing time with their peers. A distorted sense of time, reality, and social demands can isolate them and prevent them from developing relationships. "'If the choice is between a preschooler playing in a mud puddle with his neighbors or sitting in the house with a computer program,' says David Thornburg, educator and computer hardware and software designer, 'I'd far rather see him out with his friends, making discoveries with natural objects than horsing around with a computer.'"[23] A computer is just another means for self-expression and exploration of ideas.

Sometimes a computer can be the source of the comfort that comes with increased knowledge of a subject. Oren, age twelve, had kept to himself for the past few months, and his parents were worried. His mother had been diagnosed with breast cancer and had spent three months on chemotherapy after her surgery. Oren seemed to have no questions, nothing to discuss, nothing to communicate with his family. One day, his mother brought up a technical aspect of the chemotherapy, thinking it might interest him. "Oh, I know about that," was his breezy reply. "I found out all about your cancer and treatment on the computer." He had logged onto the Internet, printed out all the information he could access on breast cancer, and then found himself a support group of kids his own age in a chat room. To his credit, Oren had dealt with his concerns independently—and electronically.

5. Television and Its Friend, the VCR

THE TELEVISION PROGRAMS our children watch influence their behavior.

Linda: When Roy was four years old, he considered such television fare as Sesame Street *and* Mister Rogers' Neighborhood *to be his own special daily requirements. When friends came knocking at the door, he responded, "I can't come out to play right now, but if you want to watch my shows with me, come on in!" Excited by the new material he discovered in these shows, he would not compromise this learning time. Later, as a successful student, Roy wrote a college application essay about the importance of programs he had watched as a child.*

At its best, television can be educational and inspirational. At its worst, it can steal time from important learning experiences. Young children learn by physically doing; television can inhibit cognitive growth when it replaces those opportunities. Because nearly every household owns a television, we cannot ignore its impact on our children's lives. How can we make this a positive one?

A powerful learning tool, television can expose children to truly worthwhile experiences. Programs they watch should be within their emotional capacity and should enhance their lives beyond the television screen. From documentaries on life beneath the ocean to stories about natives of a remote island, from the design and construction of a skyscraper to the birth of a baby rhinoceros, television can provide children a window on worlds they might never otherwise encounter.

As with computers, adult involvement is pivotal. When we are aware of the programs our children watch, we can review with them what they have seen. By discussing with our children both the form and the content of what they watch, we can encourage their evaluation. Especially if we cannot be home during their television watching time, we can build into our daily conversations discussion about any television they have watched. Not only should we give our children viewing guidelines, but also we need to share these with their baby-sitters.

Children who have considered the visual components as well as the messages of what they are viewing are aware of more than just the story line; they can appreciate sound, perspective, motion, color, and composition—the art of the medium. This broader awareness often invites them to choose a greater variety of programs to watch.

Sometimes children appreciate television for the artistic value of the medium.

Sandy: *When he was young, I tried every trick I could think of to get Daniel away from the television. But like a magnet, he seemed drawn to whatever was on the screen—cartoons, movies, situation comedies. In middle school, he became interested in photography and won prizes for his work. By high school, he also began to work on films, and in college majored in visual arts. Now in his twenties, he is considering a career in film or advertising, something his mother could not have foreseen years ago. We all learn.*

Video recorders enable us to use television in the same way as books. Favorite videotaped programs can be collected into a library. They can be viewed repeatedly, slowed down, speeded up, rewound, evaluated, and analyzed like pages of poetry or literature. The availability of this wonderful resource also brings with it opportunities of questionable value. Although the movie industry provides ratings, they are no substitute for parental judgment.

When Dexter was sixteen and old enough to drive to the video store to rent his own videos, he could indulge his eclectic taste in film. Comedies, rock music videos, and thrillers all found their way to his family's television screen. For his younger siblings, his mother had to function as a sort of warden to stave off violent or inappropriate content. One Sunday, Dexter wanted to share a film with his brother and sister. His mother grilled him on the usual "no-no's." "No, Mom," he assured her. "It's just fine; there's no violence, nothing scary. It's about this boy who's a slave in the mines; then he kills his overseer and finds all this treasure. There's a bunch of blood, but it's only violent in the beginning. Don't worry, after the cave-in, he breaks out and then it's all fine."

Children can be producers as well as consumers. With access to a video camera, they can create and edit video materials. Because production involves knowledge and skilled understanding, children who have opportunities to be producers will most likely become wiser consumers.[24] This electronic medium, like the computer, thus moves out of the passive realm into the active one.

Linda: When Cliff was in middle school, he and his friends re-created on videotape what they had watched on television. They rewrote and redirected their favorite action programs to create their own versions of the exciting adventures. These productions were spiced up with homemade commercials; whoever happened to be home at the time was drafted to stardom. Once Cliff's grandmother stood in the bathroom and "advertised" toilet bowl cleaner before the lights and camera! In planning, executing, and viewing these home-crafted videos, Cliff and his friends found a productive creative outlet.

Children seem to learn from television more thoroughly than through reading or listening to radio or tape.[25] Young children accept what they view on television as reality; we can discuss and filter what our children see and help put it into a more appropriate context.[26] This is especially true of commercials, so children learn to understand the difference between what is advertising and what is part of the program.

> While TV violence has been shown to influence children negatively, there are also studies which suggest that *positive* influences result from watching *positive* behaviors on TV.
>
> —Nancy Eisenberg, *The Caring Child*
> (Cambridge, MA: Harvard University Press, 1992), p. 129

In a study for General Electric, researchers learned that after a very short time span, even as brief as thirty seconds, the brain of a television watcher goes into a mode connected with deep relaxation.[27] This is a different pattern from those related to learning a skill, physical activity, or socialization. The contrast between the brain in deep relaxation and in a more alert state reminds us that for television watching to be productive, it must be accompanied by real-life interaction. Although Saturday morning cartoons or evening situation comedies are not appropriate as a steady diet, they do serve their own valid purpose: recreation. We can help our children make choices appropriate to their specific needs.

Children who have limited exposure to written material may respond positively to learning visually.[28] Their experiences with film or television can inspire them to seek out the relevant books or periodicals. Special programs suggested by teachers can assist parents as we guide our children's television watching.

. Television can positively affect how various groups and cultures view each other and themselves. Research demonstrates that children who are members of a minority group gained "cultural pride, self-confidence, and interpersonal cooperation" when they saw members of their group portrayed in nonstereotypical ways.[29] Such programs as the long-running *Cosby* show provide a majority Caucasian culture a picture of an educated, charismatic African-American family. Another show, *The Golden Girls,* gives a light-hearted but enriched view of older people, particularly women. There is still much room on television for balanced portrayals of other less media-visible ethnic and social groups. Children's social awareness will be enhanced by more varied exposures. As the renowned commentator Edward R. Murrow observed, "'There is a great, perhaps decisive battle to be fought against ignorance, intolerance, and indifference. This weapon of television can be useful.'"[30] Like any weapon, however, television requires supervision so that its use is appropriate and constructive.

6. Multimedia

THE ENTIRE MEDIA environment is constantly changing. As technology evolves and its role in our lives expands, our children are exposed to an increasing variety of media options. From print to radio, audiotape, film, television, videotape, computers, and computerized "virtual reality," children have an arsenal of tools to employ and integrate. The social context and specific use of each can determine its impact on children's thinking. Each can also supplement and complement the others. As children learn to manipulate this technology, they are gaining abilities more diversified and wide-ranging than those of earlier eras. Their increased skills and enriched perspectives will be valuable in their changing society.

> The ideal learning environment is a multimedia one.

As the technological combinations proliferate, children can learn through more than one viewpoint. Downloading materials from the Internet, operating video cameras, and using graphing calculators for math, kids become skilled, active participants in a more sophisticated world. Electronic interactive learning is not only supplementing, but in many cases, replacing, traditional teaching approaches. Although a traditional unit on physics might have relied on a textbook, today's students can employ computer simulation, Internet resources from all over the world, and videotaped experiments performed and recorded by the students themselves. Studies of other cultures and times and all the wonders of the sciences can readily come to life before their eyes.

Youngsters must learn to process complicated, interacting bits of information quite rapidly. Their more enriched surroundings have also become more demanding. The amount of sensory input children are asked to integrate seems to increase with each electronic advance. A child's familiarity and ease with these rapid-format styles reveals a

> "While television in itself is not bad, it is the passive time spent in front of the TV that stunts the growth of [emotional intelligence] skills. . . . If you are serious about raising children with a high emotional intelligence, you must set strict limits on your child's television watching."
>
> —Lawrence E. Shapiro,
> *How to Raise a Child with a High EQ: A Parents' Guide to Emotional Intelligence* (New York: Harper Perennial, 1998), p. 35

growing acquisition of the mental dexterity and speed required to perform these tasks.

Appealing to a broad spectrum of learning styles, multimedia experiences enable children to become a part of whatever is presented. With its emphasis on sight, sound, movement, space, and action based in the present, multimedia technology can use a great number of techniques to present information. Print and radio might stimulate the imagination through their absence of visual expression; multimedia technology forces viewer participation by providing so much sensory input that the observer virtually becomes an actor.

As they learn to integrate information through a combination of media, children prepare to function in a world where rapid electronic multisensory input is a given. We are not able, even if we so desire, to put the genie back into the bottle. Our task is to familiarize ourselves with its power and discover how we can help our children benefit from its use.

TIPS TO TRY

A. Computers
   Children need:
   > access to a computer, typing skills, realistic limits on
   > computer use, and daily playtime without computers.

B. Electronic Games
   Video games can help develop:
   > flexibility, reasoning, strategizing, and thinking.

   Video games are detrimental when:
   > content is inappropriate and time spent on them
   > detracts from other activities.

C. Computer Programs
   Software offers opportunities to create through:
   > language, art, and music.

   Interactive software is best.
   Parents need guidelines to select software.

D. Using the Internet
   The Internet is a good reference source.
   E-mail is not private.
   Set up rules for use of the Internet.
   Provide guidelines for safety and length of use.

E. Television/VCR
   Television and VCR use requires adult guidance.
   Discuss with your children what they watch.
   Video recorders are creative tools.

F. Multimedia
   In a multimedia environment, children:
   > learn to process complicated interactive information
   > quickly, learn through combinations of media, and
   > need adult supervision and guidance.

GLOSSARY: WHAT IT ALL MEANS

ASCII language: a standard file format that can be read by most computers

bit: the smallest unit of information known on a computer

boot up: to turn the computer on

byte: a computer word or character composed of eight bits

CD-ROM (compact disk, read-only memory): A CD-ROM drive plays disks with text, graphics, sound, and animation. It holds a tremendous amount of information, but the user cannot change the information as on a computer disk.

chat room: a point on the Internet where people can "talk" (by typing messages) to real people in real time (not stored to be sent or received later)

clicking, dragging: terms referring to how to use computer mouse

command: an instruction transmitted to computer

computer: a machine that can receive and store information and follow instructions to manipulate, record, save, and print it

cursor: a marker or pointer on the screen showing the user's position

database: a computerized way to store, retrieve, and manipulate information

digital camera: a camera that takes photos that can be transmitted directly through a computer

disk: a flat circular surface that a computer can use to store and retrieve data

download: to use techniques to copy material communicated through a telephone line and modem from another computer onto your computer

drive: the propelling mechanism of the computer

e-mail: electronic mail sent and received by computers

folder: a directory, like a file folder, in which to store data on the computer

font: a style of lettering

graphic: a picture or image

hard copy: a printed copy of information stored on the computer

GLOSSARY

(CONTINUED)

hard drive: an electronic device on a computer used to store information in the computer

host: a computer that other computers hook up to for Internet connection

icon: a tiny picture/symbol on computer screen, used to represent locations or procedures (instead of words)

inkjet: a kind of printer that operates by squirting tiny jets of ink onto paper

Internet ("'Net"): a worldwide network of linked-together computers that can communicate with each other

keyboard: like on a typewriter, the computer's operative alphabetical, numerical, punctuation, and command keys

laser printer: the most expensive and highest-quality computer printer

load: to get a software program ready to use on a computer

memory: the part of the computer that stores data/information

menu: any list of options a user can view on a computer screen

modem (modulator/demodulator): equipment that connects a computer to a telephone line to facilitate telecommunication

monitor: the computer's screen

mouse: a small device attached to the computer or keyboard by a cable; rolled by hand, it controls the motion of a pointer (cursor) on the screen.

online: communicating on the Internet, between/among computers

password: your own secret combination of letters or numbers that lets you connect your computer with the Internet

PC (personal computer): a microcomputer priced for individual home ownership

port: a pluglike connector on the back of the computer itself, which allows for hookup with mouse, printer, and so forth

printer: the device that prints onto paper whatever the computer provides for it to do

program: the instructions written in a special language to direct the computer to perform its operations

GLOSSARY

(CONTINUED)

RAM (random access memory): a temporary place to load or store data, composing most of the internal memory of a computer

ROM (read only memory): a device that permanently holds data, making up a small part of the computer's internal memory; the user cannot change or add to ROM

save: the technique of putting a copy of what you are doing on the computer screen somewhere more permanent, such as on a disk or hard drive, so you can retrieve it later

software: the programs that tell computers what to do

sound card: a device that handles the computer's sound functions

surge protector: a device that protects a computer system from minor power fluctuations; power cords are plugged into it and it is plugged into a wall outlet

text: data in words

virus: a piece of computer code that reproduces itself within a system and can interfere with and even destroy information stored on the computer (It "contaminates" computers on the Internet and makes them "sick.")

word processing: writing, editing, and printing (if desired) text on a computer via a program/software designed for this purpose

World Wide Web: a network-wide program linking information sources throughout the Internet, using graphics and hypertext (text underlined or in color)

8

Family and School: A Partnership

ANTHONY WAS A very social and active second
grader who required a lot of attention. Although he was
academically able, he was full of energy and had a hard time
staying seated during class. His need for constant activity and
socializing was distracting to his teacher and his classmates.

An upcoming unit on Mexico provided an opportunity
for change. As part of the curriculum, the class would present
a Mexican "fiesta" for parents to enjoy. Anthony had begun
taking guitar lessons and was very proud of his progress. His
mother got permission from Anthony's teacher to have him
learn a Mexican song and perform it on his guitar for the
fiesta. Everyone was pleased with the result.

His teacher wisely expanded that experience to Anthony's
inclusion in schoolwide musical performances. Anthony was
hooked. Throughout his elementary school years, he thought
of himself as a dedicated guitar student, a mind-set that spilled
over into stronger concentration on his academic work. His
classmates began to appreciate his abilities as a musician.

On that first day of school, when we feel the wrench of a significant separation, we may heave a sigh of relief—now all that responsibility for our child's education is in professional hands. Alas, not so. Study after study confirms that parents remain the single most important factor in children's lives. Programs that involve parents produce dramatic improvements in children's motivation and success.[1] We are still raising *people*, and the school system needs to be our partner in the process. "There are three major partners in the drama of learning: the child, the school system, and the parents."[2]

> "There are three major partners in the drama of learning: the child, the school system, and the parents."

A school's most important mission is to foster the development of the individuals within it.[3] The most valuable education is learning to be the best of ourselves. *When schools help children find ways to express and develop their uniqueness, they promote individual growth.* To maintain a democracy, where we value the worth of the individual, we cannot afford to waste the talents of any member. Our obligations as mentors to nurture our children's potential is mirrored in our schools' task to provide a setting for all children to discover their strengths.[4]

In forging a partnership with our children's schools, we have a variety of approaches to use:

1. Working together
2. Providing insight
3. Formulating goals
4. Going beyond academics
5. Managing the conference

1. Working Together

JUST AS ANTHONY'S mother and teacher needed to work together to bring positive results from his talents, *all children can benefit from a home-school partnership.* In our relatively enlightened era, schools cannot do their jobs well without parents. And though our children's schools frequently reward only a limited array of special abilities, with our involvement, each child can shine.

How can parents work with the school to bring out their child's special gifts, no matter how unrelated to academics? Children who are valued for their unique qualities are children who have the confidence to improve in their areas of weakness.

Almost every major study on the subject trumpets the significance of parental involvement. One interesting endeavor is an attempt by a suburban Maryland county to put into place a program developed by James P. Comer, professor of child psychiatry at Yale University. The program aims for an atmosphere of trust and respect between parents from low-income families and their children's school, enabling parents and children to feel at ease.[5] The program's founder has a special insight into that issue; his mother, a domestic worker, saw all five of her children graduate from college.

Jacquelynn Eccles, a psychology professor at the University of Michigan, whose study encompassed 1,500 families in the Comer program, found that the "youngsters agree with their parents that parents should be involved with their children's school."[6] Just as there is no substitute for a parent's time with a child, there is no substitute for parental time spent building connections with a child's school. By becoming familiar with staff and faculty, by being on-site and by participating in activities that make up the life of the school,

> "Children need healthy communities and communities can't be healthy without the support of . . . parents."
>
> —Trish Magee,
> *Raising a Happy, Confident, Successful Child: 52 Lessons to Help Parents Grow* (Holbrook, MA: Adams Media, 1998), p. 66

we can understand the mission, philosophy, and daily operations of the institution where our child spends most of his waking hours five days a week.

There are many ways to become involved. When we choose an approach that uses our own gifts and interests, we are more likely to enjoy the experience. Of course, this is also the key to a child's success in school. Susan was a terrific organizer. After several stints managing room parent activities, she founded a parent volunteer organization and was appreciated by the entire school staff. Will was musical. He worked to bring an after-hours instrumental music program to his child's school. Patti was a nutritionist and a gifted cook. She initiated a teacher appreciation committee that provided monthly treats for the faculty. Imagine how welcome she was in school! Jerry had always been talented in math. The parent board at his sons' school asked him to be their treasurer; he initiated two programs to provide funding for school needs. Samantha loved drama, and with a houseful of boys, she especially enjoyed volunteering on the makeup committee for their school's musical production. Lisa was an avid reader. She helped launch her neighborhood school's "Great Books" program. As a parent leader, she was a weekly fixture in her children's classrooms. All of these parents were contributors to their children's schools at their convenience, using their talents.

> A supportive parent produces a supportive teacher.

Often teachers have specific suggestions for where they want help and ideas for how to provide it. To learn about our children's school experiences and social or behavioral issues, we belong—however briefly—in the classroom. There, collecting field trip permission slips, shelving books in the library corner, or helping with an end-of-unit fair or celebration, we catch glimpses of our children's lives "after the bell rings." Though our presence is just a window, more than one visit can broaden the picture we might receive from our child ("Ms. Jones always ignores me") or her teacher ("Janet spends most of her class time socializing") alone. Not only can we short-circuit potential problems, but based on our observation and involvement, we can offer helpful suggestions. Ideas have a greater potential for acceptance coming from a partner than from an adversary.

We know that children are spurred to greater academic efforts when parents are involved with their school; what our children might not tell us, but definitely feel, is pride. When a friend shows enthusiasm for our field of interest, we are complimented. When a parent gives his most valuable resource—*time*—to his child's school, it is the best of all possible gifts.

Another way to connect with our children's school is to find things going on there that we like and show our appreciation. People teaching children how to write are especially grateful for written notes; they can be saved and reread, and the authors' names are rarely forgotten. A supportive parent produces a supportive teacher.

From kindergarten through twelfth-grade commencement, when the adults who interact with our children are our allies, they will become our children's, too. Lora always made a point of meeting her children's elementary school teachers on the first day of school. Her cheery greeting and offer of help made the teachers associate her with assistance rather than with complaints. When problems arose,

> Time is the best of all possible gifts.

she could count on a thoughtful response. At the high school, she became familiar with her children's guidance counselors and was able to use them as resources, with the same friendly and encouraging approach. She became known in each school as a supportive parent and was able to advocate effectively for her children's needs. When she was unable to come to the school, she could keep in touch with teachers and counselors by telephone.

Another benefit of a parent's being there is knowledge of the school's cast of characters. One ingredient for success in a school setting is a good fit between student and teacher. A teacher with a strong authoritarian style could be intimidating to a shy, hesitant student. A teacher who is less organized and consistent than a conscientious and detail-oriented child might set up both for frustration. Some teachers enjoy lectures; others opt for emphasis on group discussion. A student who remembers best what he hears will have no trouble with the first, and a more social student will benefit from the second. An alert parent can provide accurate information to the appropriate school personnel for a productive placement. It is also useful for children to learn to cope with the problem of adapting to a specific situation that might not be able to be changed.

Linda: *When Miss Herman suddenly retired, I was distressed; my older son had had a wonderful year with this excellent teacher, and I wanted Cliff to have as enriching an experience. When I discussed the matter with the principal, I received a real-life lesson. The principal replied that she believed that each teacher brings out different qualities in a child and that the new teacher would stress different but equally valuable life skills. Interestingly, Cliff's strong interpersonal skills were first nurtured by that new teacher.*

Books, lectures, or periodicals on education can help us understand the fundamentals of how children learn and how different educational systems approach their task. If we disagree with the philosophy of a child's school, we will at least be able to understand it.

2. Providing Insight

AFTER THE CLASS has had time to settle in for the school year, and when we feel the teacher has gotten to know the students, we might take the opportunity to meet with him. We can get a general progress report (a good idea every fall) and also learn the teacher's perceptions of our child's strengths and needs. He might see things not apparent at home (especially when our daughter's door is closed, the music is on, or she is spending hours on the phone). He could be unaware of some talents not obvious between 9 A.M. and 3 P.M. (for example, our child's grace in modern dance). When teachers see beyond the academics of their students, they see them as multifaceted human beings.

Teachers can work with parents to bring a student's gifts to bear in a school setting. Becky was a quiet student who did not engage in many social activities. When her English teacher found out that she wrote short stories, she encouraged her to join the staff of the school literary magazine, a ready social group. Becky responded enthusiastically.

Max lost his dad as a youngster and had a hard early adolescence, frequently misbehaving. Through his drama teacher, he found the Drama Club to be the emotional home base he craved. He acted; he directed; he blossomed into a personable, self-confident young man.

Gary had a learning disability. He had difficulty concentrating on his schoolwork. When his parents joined a support group, they found that there was a need for educators (and parents) to hear directly from the students. A student support group was formed. Gary joined and spoke to adult gatherings throughout his high school years. His newly honed public speaking skills boosted his grades and his self-esteem.

One teacher was impressed by her student's poetry. Particularly touching was the student's stuttering problem, rendering him too embarrassed to read his own work aloud. With his teacher's long-term encouragement, this young boy overcame his speech problem; eventually, he became a professional actor, known for his rich and expressive voice. His name is James Earl Jones.[7] In all of these examples, teachers were pivotal in bringing out a student's strengths.

When we talk with our children's teachers, we need to share our goals with each other. Most teachers want their students to leave their classes more adept in life skills, to be problem solvers, individual and cooperative learners, and initiators. Parents and teachers want to promote a child's growth and development to contribute to later success.

Is it more important for Ellen's math homework to be perfect or for her to feel in command of concepts and confident in applying them to further work? How can home and school support her growth as a problem solver?

Sandy: *Jonathan paid attention to detail and was conscientious and careful in everything he did. Artistic and thorough, he frequently used long time periods for his work, both in school and out. His teachers, his dad, and I wanted to encourage his respect for his own talents but reduce his frustration level connected with his extremely high goals. We accepted his pace and supported his learning style. Now in college, he is a leader of a team of engineering students designing a solar car.*

Some thoughtful camp directors include in their camps' applications the question "What are your goals for your child this summer?" When we have to articulate our own aspirations, we have the opportunity to touch base again with our priorities.

3. Formulating Goals

WHAT KIND OF *people* do we want our children to be? How can we help our schools promote positive growth? Our own memories of school are often connected with discovering our limitations. Each of us can most likely remember when it was that we found out we could not draw or sing or play shortstop or do long division. Schools sometimes close doors instead of opening them.

> "There seems to be little correlation between high academic achievement and success in the real world."

The very traits that underlie success in life are frequently not identified in a classroom setting. The tests our children take are "not designed to test success in life."[8] What these tests *do* tend to predict is performance in their own setting: school. The pressure on students to succeed in this environment gets stronger with each decade. Students who do not produce what adults value can endure public failure and humiliation.[9] One of American education's growth industries seems to be the ubiquitous learning skills centers frequently designed to help underachievers reach their full academic potential. *When children are presented with tasks they are not developmentally ready to tackle, failure is certain.* Confronted with workbooks, homework, and tests beyond their levels of readiness, children blame themselves for their failures (they believe the adults around them must know best). How many of us are going through life convinced we are not capable in a specific subject, when perhaps it was only the result of misplaced demands? How many of us would want to pass that handicap on to our children?

Joanne's mom, discouraged in math studies in her own school years, was determined not to have her daughter repeat that experience. At fourteen, Joanne was struggling with math. Her mother began to review the homework with her nightly

"Education must concern itself with children's emotions and self-attitudes or it does not deal with the whole child. All education begins in the cradle."

—Dorothy Corkille Briggs,
Your Child's Self-Esteem (Garden City, NY: Doubleday, 1975), p. 282

and quiz her for each test. With help at home, Joanne's efforts culminated in high grades in the school's top math classes and excellent scores on standardized tests, as well. She came to regard herself as a talented math student.

Although academic standardized tests can predict academic success, they are poor overall predictors of lifetime success. They miss imagination, leadership, interpersonal, and social ability; artistic, musical, athletic or mechanical aptitude; and a practical aptitude adults call "street smarts."[10] "There seems to be little correlation between high academic achievement and success in the real world."[11]

Children with high potential in life skills might not be seen as achievers in the classroom; as mentors, their parents can have useful input. Interacting with our children daily in nonacademic settings, we are the best advocates for their potential. *Our children's teachers know only what they observe or what we tell them.*

Sometimes parents can bring to light a talent that might otherwise be hidden. Marlene was not a strong student. She had severe learning disabilities that often brought frustration to her academic work. Because her parents were supportive and informative members of her school community, Marlene's teachers found out something very special about her: she was a talented actress. The whole class knew when Marlene was in a local production, and many went to see her. Her teachers found that her performance opportunities in school enhanced her classwork. The admiration of her classmates helped preserve and expand her self-esteem.

As parents and teachers, we constantly need to appraise whether our children's environment provides opportunities to recognize their strengths.[12] Most often schools reward conformity. For some students, school years are filled with acquiring and memorizing large chunks of information, following directions, and internalizing the expectations of the system. Satisfactory completion of the standard requirements is rewarded; unusual solutions, nonconformity, or critical examination of standard truisms often are not.

If children are not adequately supported by an understanding teacher, school can be an unpleasant and uncomfortable place. How many children decline to share a new or different idea for fear it will not be acceptable? In the early elementary school years, when children can recognize the standards around them, they often lose interest in subjects if they feel they cannot perform. It should give all of us pause to reflect that the "chief instrument used [in our schools] in the search for talent is the standardized test."[13]

> It should give all of us pause to reflect that the "chief instrument used [in our schools] in the search for talent is the standardized test."

Homeschooling is an alternative some parents choose. One advantage is that the parent *is* the teacher. Standardized tests are at a minimum, and the emphasis is on the learning style of each individual child. In the home environment, a child's strengths are more easily recognized and developed. Although homeschooling can be an overwhelming responsibility for parents and sometimes an isolating peer environment for children, it has become a comfortable choice for some families.

Rhoda Kellogg wisely notes, "there is a tremendous creative impulse both in the child who eventually will become a great artist and in the child who will be a businessman or the [parent] of artists and businessmen."[14] We need to make room in our schools for them all. Mel gave up music when he was told as a child that he could not sing. Though he did lose his self-confidence in performance, he did not lose his interest in music. Many years later, he got vicarious joy when his own children played instruments and participated in choral groups.

Eileen had three musical siblings. She took piano lessons for several years, but every year her mother fired her teacher and hired a new one. Confident of Eileen's musical ability, she was sure her low level of musical proficiency was the instructor's fault. As a distinctly nonmusical adult, Eileen still enjoys music and has a piano of her own that her grandchildren use. Though neither Mel nor Eileen was especially musical, each was able to find pleasure in music.

Accountability seems to be the byword of our current educational system. We are busy; we are hassled, and we would most like to hear the "bottom line" about our children's progress in school. This results-oriented mentality transforms our schools into factories much like those in the early industrial revolution, with our students being the "products" turned out. Upon graduation, we want them to possess certain basic skills, to have acquired specific categories of fundamental knowledge, and to be competent in specific subject areas. Their grades and scores seem to be their passports into the world; little else seems to matter. Even the sportsmanship that was supposed to pervade school athletics seems to have been overtaken by the prominence of a school's win/loss record. But when these students graduate, which coaches are most lovingly remembered? Those who valued their students as *people* are the ones who stand out.

Children need respect and a sense of self-worth.

When children are asked who their heroes are, they are remarkably consistent. The adults in their lives are their role models, not the movie stars or highly paid athletes. *The people who are important to our children are those who make* them *a priority*—the parent or grandparent who has always been available, the pastor or teacher, the older brother who would sit up at night for heart-to-heart talks. When we give children our time and attention, we help them develop their skills and talents, ethics and morality. We help them become the kind of people, not products, that society needs most.

4. Going Beyond Academics

A RECENT FOCUS on community service in some school districts has given children an opportunity to widen their vision of the world. Children whose strengths lie in social awareness, empathy, interpersonal relationships, leadership, or organizational skills can shine in such endeavors.

Creative thinkers can also find new ways to address old ills. Trudy, a talented actress and dancer, organized a dramatic troupe to present shows at nursing homes and hospitals. Arlene, working on her conversational Spanish, founded a bilingual tutoring service for her city's Hispanic community.

Pierce, who liked action and enjoyed being around people, worked for three years as a volunteer medic with the local rescue squad. None of these students were academic stars. But all of them were developing stellar life skills.

Schools that enrich their pupils with such real-life opportunities allow their children to grow. Schools either give children an understanding that they *can* do well, or they convey an underlying feeling of inferiority. As with Trudy, Arlene, and Pierce, a school program can highlight the importance of life talents to our society.

Parents can encourage schools to be flexible and emphasize individual contributions. Spotlighting a child's particular talent in a classroom builds her sense of self-reliance and self-sufficiency. Children need respect and a sense of self-worth.[15] The repercussions from these experiences is sometimes astonishing.

Children who feel valued are children likely to succeed. A gangly, perky young teenager had an average academic record when she entered her public high school. The school, it turned out, had more than its share of academic superstars, but it also rewarded dramatic, musical, and athletic talent with high-profile exposure. The school was especially known in the local area for the high caliber of its dramatic and musical productions. The teenager, a talented actress, had found herself a "home." Her name was Goldie Hawn.

A father's missionary postings forced such frequent family moves that his wife devised a novel way to stimulate and pacify their children. Everywhere they settled, the children were tutored by resident craftspeople especially talented in skills specific to their locality. Among other things, the youngsters learned basketry, woodcarving, and weaving. In adulthood, one daughter found these windows on other cultures to be valuable experiences for her life. Her name was Margaret Mead.

Because each child has unique potential, our job as parents is to help teachers recognize her abilities. This prescription is a tall order for a class of thirty or more students and a curriculum demanding accountability through periodic standardized testing. How can a well-meaning parent help a well-meaning teacher? Often a child's special skills can enhance a class unit of study.

Once we are aware of what our children are studying, we can suggest enrichment ideas. A talented seamstress, ten-year-old Fran made beautifully costumed dolls for a unit on Native Americans. Ezra's math teacher captured the imagination of his sports fans by having teams of students work out statistics on batting averages or league standings. Marie's terrarium was especially welcome in her science unit on botany. Eight-year-old Alvin was very proud of his box of mounted insects. His teacher wisely included his work in a unit on the environment.

From even a brief time spent in the classroom, we can imagine what kinds of activities might appropriately draw on our children's strengths. Those whose talents tend toward interpersonal, organizational, and leadership skills can make a contribution through group projects, peer activities, panels, seminars, and student government. A detail-oriented, conscientious, quiet student might thrive on individual research projects. Volunteering in the office at her daughter's school, Rita was available when the opportunity arose to run their new Junior Achievement program. She enjoyed helping the students learn the principles of business and finance, of special interest to her child. If our child is an outdoor person, we might offer to help develop an outdoor education program. Children with athletic, social, and science-oriented skills can become class stars in nonclassroom settings. Sometimes a child who seems unequipped for such out-of-the-classroom activities surprises everyone, even herself.

Sandy: Stephen was a cerebral fifth grader. He considered a walk from the classroom to the school bus to be exercise. He routinely opted out of recess games, preferring to read or play chess. He was less than thrilled anticipating the class's four-day trip to an outdoor education site. But afterward the photos the teachers brought back spoke for themselves. There were pictures of Stephen, helmeted and harnessed, rappelling down a breathtaking cliff; Stephen pulling himself on a zipline across a gaping ravine; Stephen leading a group of classmates up the steep terrain of a rocky hillside. When the class returned to school, the students, the teacher (and Stephen himself) saw him as a very different person.

Sometimes a child's abilities are not obvious, inside or outside the classroom. But with a variety of opportunities, new strengths might emerge. An observant teacher builds on those skills in the classroom. A sense of competence ignites a child's ability to learn.

FOUR STEPS TO PREPARE FOR A SUCCESSFUL CONFERENCE

1. Identify any problems.
2. Set a goal.
3. Collect relevant information.
4. Contact the teacher in a pleasant way.

5. Managing the Conference

CHILDREN'S BRAINS ARE programmed to learn perhaps their most difficult tasks without any apprenticeship or formal instruction. By the time they are eighteen to twenty-four months old, nearly all children can walk and make themselves understood in their native language, whether it is Swahili or Mandarin Chinese. As parents, we appreciate their efforts and reward whatever they accomplish. Unfortunately, this individual pace of learning and reinforcement is rarely duplicated in school. Competition, standardized testing, grades, deadlines, boredom, unappealing texts, student labeling, and burned-out teachers all effectively poison a child's learning environment. The enthusiastic walker or talker may have metamorphosed into the homework slacker, the daydreamer, or the teen majoring in telephone. Every tuned-out, turned-off child is a stressed-out child. If we can help reduce our child's stress and support his talents, we will enable him to approach future stresses with greater resources.

When we see signs of stress, we need to trace them to the root cause to effect change. Is the culprit a lack of skills, a lack of self-confidence, or a vicious circle, one feeding on the other? In an entire system that is *product* rather than *process* oriented, and geared to a "bottom line" mentality, everyone is under stress. An atmosphere of pressure fosters egocentric behavior. No one can focus clearly on the needs or concerns of others. When teachers are driven by results instead of approaching learning developmentally, enrichment suffers. No one can practice James Thurber's wonderful maxim: "It's better to know some of the questions than all of the answers."[16] *When pressure is taken off schools, pressure is taken off children.*

What do we do when confronted with the dreaded "vicious circle"? It is critical that parents are "informed, involved advocates for our children."[17] The solution frequently begins with a conference, a meeting with the teachers. No matter how inconvenient, it is essential that we manage to get ourselves *to* the conference. For important concerns, there is no substitute for a face-to-face meeting with the teacher.

We should approach our encounter with the same mind-set we would have for any business meeting. We need to map out our goals in advance and list our questions, concerns, and suggestions. If we have a plan of action to request, we should work with the teacher to build in a timetable for feedback. Meeting with the teacher as a coworker who shares the same desired result keeps the process positive. Any complaints about school should be the subject of discussion with the teacher, not with the child.[18] Some parents are more likely than others to gain results from a conference. Most professionals (in any discipline) will respond to a person who interacts in a friendly and inquiring manner. Successful parents understand that the adults involved need to pool their ideas and resources to address a child's problem.

> Our children can learn an important life lesson: that problems can have solutions.

As in any productive meeting, a positive attitude on the part of all members is important. Contact with the teacher can begin by asking when he could meet to talk over some concerns about the child. When we sit down together, an opening compliment is a wonderful and effective icebreaker, even if it is just an acknowledgment of the teacher's long day and hard work, big class load, and so forth. Any specific positive statement we can make ("We love your quarterly newsletter about the social studies units"; "That bridge-building assignment for math was such a clever idea.") will let the teacher know we have not arrived for a lynching.

Watching for eye contact (keep it direct) and body language gives clues to how comments and questions are being received. When we present the issue as our *child's* problem, we immediately take the teacher off the defensive and into a listening mode. Even if the problem seems to be caused by a teacher's inappropriate behavior, we can couch our approach in our child's perceptions, unhappiness, or discomfort. Then the task is making our child feel better, rather than evaluating the teacher's unacceptable behavior.

COMPONENTS OF A POSITIVE CONFERENCE

1. Interact with the teacher in a respectful and supportive manner.
2. Clearly state the problem in language that indicates a willingness to work with the teacher.
3. Present supporting facts to clarify the issue.
4. Ask how the teacher sees the problem.
5. Ask the teacher what ideas he has for a solution and what input he would like from parents.
6. Offer supportive suggestions.
7. Devise a plan of action together.
8. Build in a timetable for feedback and results.
9. Express appreciation for the teacher's time and help.

Once we define the problem, our next step is to present our goal: improvement in math grades, better skills working with peers, enhanced confidence in essay writing. Any information we have to clarify the situation is helpful. ("Bert never seems to understand his homework." "Judy is always reluctant to talk about the project with any of her committee members." "No matter how much work Bill puts into his writing, he always tells us he feels it isn't good enough.") As the teacher is getting a clearer picture of what we are observing, she begins to relate that information to her own perceptions. When we ask for her opinion, we show respect for her ability as an educator. When we ask for her ideas in finding a solution, we remind her of her importance in the problem-solving process. By offering supportive suggestions and assistance outside the classroom, we emphasize joint ownership of our child's education. We can conclude with a mutually comfortable timetable for feedback, through a conference, phone call, or a note sent home. A time frame for meeting the goal may be premature, but if it seems appropriate, we can broach that issue. Closing the meeting with a genuine appreciation of the teacher's efforts and a promise to back her up at home further motivates the teacher. People do wish to please those who seem to be on their side.

This scenario can have a less-than-happy outcome when a teacher has no grasp of the problem or is reluctant to provide information. Demands, threats, unsubstantiated claims, or attacks on a teacher's performance never work. The problem remains and festers.

Solving problems requires that we be our child's advocate. "Why can't I do this math, Mom?" sobbed Cary as he once again struggled with his homework. "The teacher says I know it!" When Cary's mom investigated the problem, she learned that when he lost his third-grade math book earlier that week, the teacher replaced it with a fourth-grade book and advanced him to the next group for math; she had run out of third-grade books. Advocating for her child, his mother insisted to the principal that a third-grade math book had to be found for Cary. Once he was made aware of the problem, the principal saw to it that Cary had the appropriate book.

In such cases it is time for us to march up the chain of command and see the principal. We can proceed with the same steps as in the previous conference, assured in the likelihood that the principal has most likely heard the problem before. The principal has probably discussed this issue many times. We need to *listen*. As we discuss the situation, we can make it clear that we are looking for ways to defuse it. Especially if a child's experience is negatively affecting her self-image or her attitude toward school, an intervention is vital. We can request the suggestions of a school counselor, a coach, an area supervisor, or another expert within the system. The majority of professionals in education are in their jobs because they care deeply about children. With some clear communication, we can alleviate school problems. And our children will learn an important life lesson: that problems can have solutions.

TIPS TO TRY

A. Partnership
   Parents are:
      the most important factor in children's education and
      responsible for developing a relationship with school.

B. Working Together
   Parents should:
      visit the school, meet the teacher, and become
      involved in a way you enjoy.

C. Providing Insight
   Remember to:
      tell the teacher your child's strengths and suggest how
      your child's talents can be tapped at school.

D. Formulating Goals
   Effective goal setting involves:
      establishing goals for the school year and reevaluating
      how school is working for your child.

E. Going Beyond Academics
   Parents can:
      suggest enrichment ideas to the teacher and
      encourage creativity.

F. Managing the Conference
   Try to:
      request a conference if you sense any problems at
      school, prepare for conferences in advance, approach
      the teacher with a positive attitude, formulate goals
      together, and plan for follow-up.

9

After the Bell Rings

M S. SAUNDERS'S MUSIC class was having a unit on international music. The sixth-graders learned about the music and instruments of non-Western cultures and the significance of musical traditions in the history of a society. They learned some non-Western melodic scales and tried to build some musical instruments used in other countries. Dove, who usually had trouble focusing on class lessons, began to tune in. He loved the "talking drum" of Ghana and tried to manipulate it to imitate language. The sitar, a relative to his beloved guitar, fascinated him. He tried his hand at sight-reading a Chinese melody on the xylophone and began composing music that echoed some of the traditions he had discovered. A class where he was often distracted now appealed to his energy, creativity, and musical ability.

"Every child already possesses what it takes to think, to ask questions, learn and create."[1] What environment best supports our children's continued self-discovery? What kind of learning atmosphere is the best incubator for the resilient, problem-solving innovators our society needs? What setting best nurtures talents that can adapt to a future whose only certainty is change?

In previous eras, the traditional skills (reading, writing, mathematics) made up the necessary prerequisites for many jobs. Other skills, once acquired, were employed as long as we worked. The subjects our children now pursue and the jobs they will train for might be replaced entirely by disciplines unheard of today. As their mentors, the most important training we can give our children is the ability to communicate.

> "Every child already possesses what it takes to think, to ask questions, learn and create."

The world our children will face will be a smaller one than we have known. The progress of telecommunications and information systems enables people from nearly every spot on the globe to be in easy communication. We will need, among other assets, increased understanding of cultures outside of those in our comfort zone. Our children must be adaptable, curious, and empathic. They will need more interpersonal skills, even from their perch at a computer screen. They will need the language skills to make themselves understood and to reflect back their comprehension of another's point of view. *In an age of accelerated technology, they will need accelerated communication skills.*

"I like to work with people" is a common job questionnaire response. We can develop and support talent in interpersonal relationships. Candace, a fourth-grader whose assertiveness sometimes interfered with smooth peer relations, spent her summer in a camp for children from many cultures. She described a new friend's customs: "They do it differently there, Mom. I don't agree, but it's their way and we can't criticize." She wants a job that takes her to other countries when she is grown.

Inside and outside school, children's experiences are related like fragments of a mosaic. What they encounter outside class colors their perspective on their world. It enriches who they are as people. Their school experiences add more pieces to their picture.

As parents we need to be aware of:

1. Cooperative learning

2. Individual learning

3. Outside talents inside school

4. Special gifts

5. Risk taking and creativity

6. Evaluating our schools

1. Cooperative Learning

Cooperative learning can be a positive tool for developing more than academic skills. Harris, quiet and tentative with his peers, found that his family's stay in Africa gave him special status when his class studied the customs of that country. His teachers gave him time to talk to the class about his experiences and featured his artifacts in class displays. His new confidence helped his friendships grow.

A popular unit for one school's fifth grade is the study of America's westward movement. Students become part of wagon train teams and take the roles of real or fictional historic characters. According to the circumstances each team confronts (through random drawings of "situation cards"), the students must adapt and succeed in their journey. Flexibility, ingenuity, and interpersonal skills are at a premium in this setting. The teachers wisely use this format to group students with complementary skills. The team that wins is the one that has made the most productive use of each member's strengths. New combinations of leaders and followers, organizers and empathizers, often produce new abilities and new respect among the participants. This is a game of skill building in every sense of the term.

Regardless of cultural backgrounds, a school setting is structured to help children interact in socially acceptable patterns. When children enter kindergarten, they are exposed to group situations, from the inevitable social role playing of "house" or "fort" to the more project-oriented focus of block building or bug collecting. When students are encouraged to work together and to resolve their problems together, they develop pride in their social skills.

Children whose talents lie in interpersonal relations have an opportunity to cooperate in a learning environment. Not only leaders and managers, but organizers, good listeners, and strategists can shine in a setting emphasizing cooperative tasks. Teachers grouping children whose styles complement each other foster improved peer interactions. The members of Mr. Walden's sixth-grade math class eagerly anticipated their toothpick bridge-building project. They divided into groups of four and began to organize. Each student took a job: one was the chief architect; one, the accountant; another, the carpenter; and the fourth, project director. Each member produced a scale drawing of his own bridge design;  the team then decided on a final design for construction. They "purchased" lumber, welding supplies, and land using their fictional budget of $1.5 million. After the bridges were displayed, they were load-tested to determine their load-to-mass ratios. Every student had a personal investment of ideas, time, and energy in the group's project.

In the other disciplines, cooperative efforts often highlight talents of each group member. The artist, the amateur geologist, the model builder all have strengths to contribute to a group. Interpersonal traits frequently are the most appreciated.

The student who is organized and detail oriented will shine by keeping the whole group on task. The natural manager will maintain an overview of the entire project and encourage a productive outcome from each member. The empathic listener may be the most valued team member, as he irons out problems and facilitates constructive working relationships.

A successful group is built on the strengths of its individual members. The staff of a small independent school had a transforming summer experience. They attended an outdoor education program that required them to work as a team to find and recover an ancient skull. Because clues were hidden in hazardous places, the participants traveled by land and water, hiking, kayaking, and climbing up steep precipices. As a group, they were committed to risk taking and mutual support to reach their common goal. Their ability to achieve as a group, built on their individual strengths, resulted in their success. The self-confidence and mutual respect the teachers gained from their adventure changed their way of looking at each other and at their teaching. They entered their classrooms that fall with a commitment to experiences that would highlight each student's untapped strengths. They were determined to unearth those talents in a group environment just as they had unearthed the ancient skull together.[2]

> A student is not a cup for knowledge or talent to be poured into. She is a member of a learning team; the teacher is the coach.

2. Individual Learning

In a setting that values an individualized approach, students have a wonderful chance to be noticed for their strengths. Teachers who recognize that students each have a different pace will be patient as youngsters acquire their skills at different times and in different ways. One child might learn to read at age two, while another might not be able to decode written language until age seven. By ten or eleven, both can be capable readers. Progress in a child's development rarely comes in even stages.

From stories of such famous athletes as Michael Jordan, who at first failed to make his high school basketball team, we are reminded that talent takes time and attention to nurture. When children are taught to adapt, to compensate, to work in the way they function best, they make room for their strengths to come alive. Kristi Yamaguchi, the Olympic gold medal figure skater, began life as a club-footed baby. The legendary runner Wilma Rudolph was a youthful polio victim before she began running to build her strength.

When adults see children in positive ways, children mirror that vision. Jaime Escalante, the Los Angeles physics teacher made famous in the movie *Stand and Deliver,* reminds us that if we expect our children to succeed, they will.[3] Sonia was intimidated by the large high school she entered as a tenth grader. She sat in the back of her English class and doodled or wrote bits of poetry in her notebook. Her teacher, noticing her writing, worked together with her to submit a poem to a national student writing magazine. Later, when her class read the current issue, Sonia recognized her own poem. With increased self-confidence, she began to write for the school literary magazine and went on to major in writing in college.

Nine-year-old Ames seemed to have a nose for trouble. Whenever he thought something was unjust, he felt it was his duty to speak out, a trait that did not endear him to his teachers. Then he entered Ms. Risner's drama class. She talked about Shakespeare; she gave the class exercises with character roles, and Ames chose an ethnic one with an accent. Ms. Risner complimented him on his work. With some surprise and delight, he confided, "I'm not even afraid in front of an audience; I think I'm really *good* at this!" He never had a behavior problem with Ms. Risner.

"Personal attention and interest from a teacher can be a powerful motivator."

—Peter L. Benson, Judy Galbraith, and Pamela Espeland,
*What Kids Need to Succeed: Proven, Practical Ways
to Raise Good Kids* (Minneapolis: Free Spirit, 1994), p. 89.

When five-year-old Lawrence entered kindergarten, he was nervous and awkward with his classmates. His physical development was slow, so he could not play most games at recess and found himself alone, usually reading a book. His principal, Mrs. James, knew all about him and understood. She took him out of class for his first visit to the school library. "You may pick out any book you want," she smiled. That day, he came home with a book and a smile of his own. Sonia, Ames, and Lawrence all blossomed when adults recognized and supported their strengths.

Because individuals vary in their pacing and in the ways they pursue their goals, children need teachers who view success as a culmination of repeated efforts. As we held our child's hand and then let go as he took those wobbly first steps, a good teacher gives each student the necessary support and then allows him to take his own wobbly steps toward his goal. When our six-year-old ricochets along without her bicycle training wheels, we praise the accomplishment. When she falls, we know it is not a permanent condition. With our encouragement and our children's own drive, they, and we, have no doubt about their eventual success. They need the same emotional foundation at school.

When children are given an opportunity to formulate their own goals, understand their own problems, and work out their own methods of addressing them, they acquire ownership of their journey toward success. A student is not a cup for knowledge or talent to be poured into. She is a member of a learning team; the teacher is the coach. A good teacher "doesn't tell students what they should know, but helps them pose their questions and find their own answers."[4]

Linda: Aaron, smart and multitalented, had a lot of friends in middle school but lacked self-assurance. Then a teacher assigned a research paper, and he had an idea. He received permission to substitute a video production for a written project and borrowed a video camera. He wrote his own script, rounded up family members and friends as cast and camera crew, and served as talent, producer, director, and editor all at the same time. The show was an instant hit. The formerly self-conscious child went on to many more creative projects and to starring musical roles in high school and college. We were all fortunate that Aaron had teachers who were supportive of his innovative approach; I did not have to get involved in advocating for his creative efforts.

3. Outside Talents Inside School

We call our schools "halls of learning." How ironic it is that before our children enter school they have probably done their most important learning.[5] They have become competent in their native language; they have learned to use their bodies efficiently: to feed themselves, to walk, to climb, to run, and even to balance on a bicycle or roller skates. They have learned colors, numbers, and basic cause-and-effect reasoning; they can do puzzles and memorize songs. The methods we adults use to "help" our children learn usually are very unlike those that our children have been using naturally and comfortably until kindergarten. Often the results of our trying to graft our preferred style onto theirs are humiliation, frustration, and fear. *If as parents we can tune in more to the ways children pursue knowledge on their own, we can know better how to help them shine in school.*

If we were to secretly watch several children at the same task, we would get a feel for their differences, and the surprising uniformity, of their approaches. Five-year-old Jamie chose his blocks carefully; he patiently assembled construction in a pattern already formed in his head. Melanie just experimented with whatever was on hand, letting the variety of sizes and shapes of her blocks dictate her creation. Neither would ever have thought a teacher's lecture on block building especially helpful, and neither would have welcomed a kind-hearted adult attempt to assist them in their work. They expected and accepted autonomy without a second thought. A primary goal of our school systems should be to encourage children to develop their own abilities.

> Motivation is the strongest ingredient in learning.

Left to proceed at their own pace, children often are satisfied with the results of their efforts. In their "instinct of workmanship," discussed by the noted educator John Holt, children want their creations done as well as they can make them, not to please anyone else but themselves.[6] As we involve them in a variety of disciplines, we need to offer them opportunities to choose what is most meaningful to them. Children will pursue an idea or skill that appeals to their innate drive to make sense of their world, whether the subject at hand is government, poetry, or cell biology. They learn in spurts; *a child's development usually proceeds unevenly.* As long as he is excited by his task, he is apt to cover substantial ground on his own.

Sandy: *Beginning when Jonathan was eleven, he liked to build model airplanes. He collected books about airplanes and stored pieces of balsa wood that he cut to his own designs. He*

> "It is not always necessary to be right."
>
> —John Holt,
> *How Children Learn* (New York: Dell, 1967), p. 91

read about drag and lift and started making notes on graph paper about the properties and probable performance of his own creations. When his science classes studied gravity and motion, he was in his element. He continued his work on his own time. His meticulous style lent itself naturally to his subject. By the time he reached high school physics class, he was doing outstanding work. Supported with equipment and supplies he needed and left alone to pursue his own interests, Jonathan was able to expand and develop them to his own satisfaction.

The ways our children experience subject learning will determine whether they feel skilled and competent or frustrated and fearful. When schools encourage individual approaches to competence from a broad menu of disciplines, they support just the kind of creative drive that nurtures children's most natural way of learning.

A child's learning—in his unique style—never boxes him in; it leads him to approach a wider world.[7] The sixth-grade English class was reading a book that told of friction between two fictional groups living and selling their wares on the Lower East Side of New York City at the end of the nineteenth century. Their drama class worked on character acting, accents, period costumes, and stage settings. Their social studies class discussed economics, competition, and the stock exchange, which naturally spilled over into math class. The students formed fictional cookie baking companies and had to incorporate, along with a business plan, a budget and marketing strategy. They had to design, implement, and sell their products and produce their own advertising. One group decided that their sales would increase with some giveaways, so they had a designated team member purchase prizes from their marketing budget. On their own, several children did further research on real stocks and began to do some real-life investing. Science class worked on consumer education and scientific team-testing of properties claimed by various products. In each area, different students excelled. An outspoken one loved drama, a careful researcher enjoyed product testing, a mathematical thinker loved the economic models, and a budding entrepreneur could not wait to read the daily stock quotes and make his own investments. What is enjoyable is retained. When possible, teachers need to seize opportunities to present subjects incorporating a variety of methods. *When children are offered the chance to learn using their individual abilities, they are more likely to succeed.*

4. Special Gifts

Inevitably, parents and schools must deal with treatment of children with special talents. "'I was different. I was always different. Why didn't anybody notice me?'" exclaimed John Lennon (of the Beatles).[8] What is the responsibility of the school to a youngster of special gifts? In his book *What Kids Need to Succeed*, Peter L. Benson reminds teachers and administrators to expect their students to succeed, expose students to positive role models whose backgrounds are similar, build into the school year recognition rituals for all kinds of talents, and help students develop their own assets.[9]

> "There is nothing so unequal as the equal treatment of unequals."

Research confirms that gifted individuals usually have more than one special talent.[10] Teachers who coach after-school sports routinely enjoy getting to know students in new settings. Often leadership and dependability, seen on the playing field, surface in the classroom. A teacher pegging a child as a math whiz needs to

"My parents [Sargent and Eunice Kennedy Shriver] were strong consistent role models for me. They were supportive of my efforts, no matter how well (or poorly) I did. [But] they made it clear that if you *could* do well, you were to do well."

—Mark Shriver,

state congressional delegate (D-Maryland), interview with authors,

July 8, 1998

know he is also a dedicated musician. What John Gardner calls the "tyranny of talent" should not force any child into an early and restrictive mold.[11]

By tapping into a wide variety of strengths, a teacher can support abilities while continuing to give every student the opportunity to grow. "There is nothing so unequal as the equal treatment of unequals." [12] Talents that are encouraged grow. When we allow children many enriching experiences, we permit them to enjoy all of their abilities. The danger in a too-narrow focus is that it forces both the child and his peers to think of him as one-dimensional. Even later in life, a second or third talent may be the one that makes the pressure of a life work bearable. Winston Churchill's landscape paintings gave him a peaceful island during his most trying periods. Thomas Jefferson was an avid naturalist who cherished his collections at Monticello. The painter Charles W. Peale was a botanist of major repute, and Albert Schweitzer was a concert-level pianist before his work in medicine made him famous.

One of the interesting characteristics of talent is that each skill has its own developmental timetable. Abilities are "plastic"—they can be modified and molded; they grow and change over time.[13] A child who emphasizes one of her talents might focus on a different one later.

Sandy: Stephen had immersed himself in science since third grade. He loved to think about chemical reactions and, later, genetics and biochemistry. As he grew older, he anticipated a career in biochemical research. But all through his school years he also wrote, first, comic books, fantasy, and science fiction stories and, later, in high school, poetry. For him, relaxation was setting some of his poems to music. A favorite high school teacher was a poet who encouraged Stephen. Happy to see his poems in the school literary magazine, Stephen soon became a staff member. In college, the professor who mentored him was a literary critic; she helped him develop his writing further. Though his early interest was science, he has chosen writing as a career.

Harper also loved to write; he wrote for his school literary magazines. But he also loved math. In his spare time, he thought about numbers and their relationships; he formulated problems and tried to solve them. His science projects always revolved around numbers. In college, he took math courses and wrote for the literary magazines; he even founded a magazine. In the end, math won. Harper is now a college mathematics professor.

William was a talented musician. He played saxophone all through high school and enjoyed jamming with friends in college. A turning point for him was choosing between a career in music or a career in government, his other focus. He chose government and later became our forty-second president. Who knows what would have happened if Bill Clinton had been directed otherwise?

Because a child's talents continue to grow and change, a school's evaluation of his abilities also needs to be a "continuing process."[14] Parents can help foster flexibility by maintaining regular contact with teachers. Providing the teacher information about our children's activities and experiences, we can also learn about their classrooms. This is part of our job as mentors. In high school, teachers appreciate (and are often surprised by) information parents provide about a student's special interests. *If every child were treated as gifted, schools could resolve many educational problems.*[15]

5. Risk Taking and Creativity

From the time a toddler takes her daring first steps until she lands at a school desk, she has learned to challenge and experiment. She has tried different methods to attain the skills necessary for daily living. She is eager to continue to explore her world and master new possibilities. "Creativity is a natural endowment that is present in . . . all children."[16] Then something happens. She learns that most things in school have one *right* way of being done. She raises her hand only when she has the *right* answer. She learns to be cautious, to wait, to be told what to do, how to approach a new situation, to be evaluated by others on her abilities. She learns that by taking risks she risks failure.

A second-grade math lesson involved measurement. The teacher encouraged the class to guess how many yards long the longest wall was, how many feet made up the length of a windowsill. The class was quiet. No one wanted to guess; no one wanted to be wrong.

There is an inherent tension in our educational system. We send children to school to civilize them into society's expectations. They need to learn to share, pay attention, take turns, and be responsible, considerate members of a group. We want children to acquire academic skills, too, to be able to reason, problem-solve, and apply concepts learned in a variety of settings. Yet the skills we teach them stress convergent, rather than divergent, thinking. Getting the right answer is frequently more important than asking the right question. *Creativity, the gift that society needs most, derives from* divergent *thinking,* the kind that wanders off to the left of the discussion and wonders, "What would happen if . . . ?" The daydreamers, the intense thinkers, the incessant project planners are often the creative thinkers in a class. By supporting risk taking, a school is supporting innovation and initiative.

Too often when creativity and conformity clash, conformity wins. What can parents do to support divergent thinking, especially after our children have entered school? When we raise children who are not afraid to hazard their opinions, who are applauded for seeing things in new ways, tackling problems of their own design, reaching out to areas and skills beyond the familiar, we develop creative thinkers. Often innovators are so busy with the next project that they have forgotten all about the one they just completed; this is where parents can help. A reminder about the relevance of a child's work to a unit in school or a discussion with the teacher about an ongoing project can be beneficial for all. The child is reinforced for ingenuity, the teacher has enriched her classroom unit, and the rest of the class has observed a positive result of risk taking.

In the right setting, divergent thinking can be contagious. Eleven-year-olds Francis, Hal, and Gus considered themselves the "ecology rangers." In their spare time, they designed and implemented innovative solutions for keeping

> "Highly creative elementary children often become school problems."
>
> —Cheri Fuller,
> *Unlocking Your Child's Learning Potential* (Colorado Springs: Navpress, 1994), p. 126

their neighborhood cleaner and less hazardous. When their class began to study environmental protection, the boys were prepared. Their recycling and conservation efforts stimulated exciting ideas from their class.

If children feel it is safe to think and act creatively, they model for each other the benefits of innovative thinking. They accept failure as a natural component of success and are not concerned with their lack of expertise as they tackle challenges.[17] They retain within themselves the excitement of learning because they are not afraid to step into the unknown. Continuing to grow and learn for a lifetime, they are the ones who move society forward. "If we are careful not to push a child beyond the limits of his courage, he is almost sure to get braver."[18]

6. Evaluating Our Schools

One of the hardest jobs a parent does is send a child off to school. Of the separations they have experienced together, this can be the one most fraught with anxieties. The child wonders what this new place has in store for her; as parents, we wonder how she will fare in this bigger, more impersonal world. Compounding the worry is our uncertainty about the new environment. Does it resemble the school we remember? Does it operate on a philosophy we have never heard of? Will our child fit in? How can we tell? How do we know whether we have made the right match? In the context of supporting and developing our child's strengths, how can we best evaluate her school?

The most comforting information we can begin with is that we know our child and we know ourselves. We begin and end as partners in the educational odyssey, so a school should satisfy the basic needs of both. When children enter school, they enter society. What kinds of messages are we sending them?

SUPPORTING A CHILD'S TALENTS IN SCHOOL: TEN QUESTIONS TO ASK

1. Does the building feel welcoming?

2. Are the students active or passive?

3. Does the curriculum encourage children to think?

4. Are students' skills shared with the class?

5. Is there time to explore?

6. Is the subject presented from a variety of viewpoints?

7. Is there a mixture of ways the students can learn?

8. Is parent involvement encouraged?

9. Do teachers seem to appreciate students' special skills?

10. Do the students fell valued?

Supporting a Child's Talents in School: Ten Questions to Ask

1. *Does the building feel welcoming?*

To assess a school, we must visit the building during class hours. We need to be in the school building *during* school hours *before* our child enrolls. Only by seeing what happens there can we make adequate judgments about the program and the people who run it. A staff inhospitable to adult visitors is likely to be uneasy about children, too. If it feels inviting to us, it probably will for our child. A welcoming environment does not have to be new and fancy; bright colors, bulletin boards or walls

filled with the work of children, from elementary
school even through high school, indicate that the
staff values what the students produce. A display of
the work of only one or two students reveals poor
support for those who do not meet specific standards. *Children, like adults, need to feel their efforts
are valued.* In many subject areas, children are
unnecessarily ranked and are too often discouraged
by the judgments of adults. Standards often backfire; Charles Schultz's (*Peanuts'* creator) drawings,
for example, were rejected by his high school
yearbook staff. If the setting seems too sterile, it
may be that the teachers do not have the time to do
more with their rooms and hallways. Volunteering
once a month to post students' work or decorate
bulletin boards is one way to help.

2. *Are the students active or passive?*

Are they involved in hands-on experiences? Are
the students participants in the learning process, or
are they seen as vessels to be filled up? Sometimes a
classroom seating pattern might give a clue: schools
with room after room of unending rows of desks can
be places where students are expected to interact by
raising their hands at the right time and giving the
expected answers. A variety of seating arrangements,
activity centers, clusters of students working together
reveal a school's activist approach to learning.

3. *Does the curriculum encourage children to think?*

Respecting children who postulate ideas and
solutions for themselves gives them the most
important gift in their education. A curriculum
with emphasis solely on information gathering
severely limits the development of a child's talent.
"Imagination is more important than knowledge,"
was the dictum of Albert Einstein.[19] If you cannot

influence the curriculum, you can enrich it through volunteering. After-hours activities based on parents' experiences and talents can open up exciting possibilities for students. Book clubs, biking groups, sports skills clubs, cooking groups, and movie clubs are examples.

4. *Are students' skills shared with the class?*

Performance opportunities on a regular basis, skill demonstrations, products fashioned independently, and student teaching experiences are all ways students can showcase their abilities in a school setting. Schools that regularly feature their students' work send a message of pride in all of their members. Often such exposure stimulates classmates to take up a new interest or learn a related skill. We can volunteer our own expertise in areas from organization and note taking to communication skills or music.

5. *Is there time to explore?*

What is a day like in school? Is there a rigid schedule? Are conversations stopped abruptly? Does a teacher have the flexibility to devote an entire class period to something interesting that "just came up"? When students feel they have time to explore their materials and ideas, they are given fertile ground for creativity. When children come up with their own problems and their own solutions, they acquire ownership of their subject and move more confidently to mastery. Sometimes a teacher needs help in the classroom to free her time for working with individual children. Contact your child's teacher and ask what improvements she would like to see in the classroom. How can you help?

6. *Is a subject presented from a variety of viewpoints?*

    A music course, for example, could include a unit on unusual instruments or ancient ethnic tonal scales and patterns. When students receive the message that many approaches are available to them, they feel free to make their own choices.

7. *Is there a mixture of ways the students can learn?*

    Use of groups, teams, and partnerships as well as individual work reminds children that they can learn *from* as well as *with* a peer. Use of students' creative abilities, imaginative approaches, and sensory input all provide an enriched learning environment.

8. *Is parent involvement encouraged?*

    Are teachers available to talk with parents? Are times set aside for face-to-face parent-teacher conferences? When teachers are flexible and welcoming to parents, communication is usually positive and productive. *When parent involvement in a school is encouraged, everyone benefits.* If parents are not involved, you need to find out why. Meet with your child's principal and find out how parents can be helpful. Holding special "subject fairs" on weekends or school holidays can highlight children's talents. Street-type celebrations can spotlight art, music, drama, dance, languages, and other cultures.

9. *Do teachers seem to appreciate students' special skills?*

    Is there evidence that teachers take an interest in each child's abilities? Do teachers give individual attention or provide for a child to use his strengths in a class setting? Skills in leadership, visual arts, organization, and writing are often easy to highlight and spot in a classroom. Does the teacher appear to take advantage of the diversity of his students' talents?

10. *Do the students feel valued?*

Body language, facial expressions, and interactions in the classroom are quick giveaways here. Is it a lively, interesting place? Do students seem eager to participate? Do they expect to be included? Children who look forward to school most days and who feel connected in a positive way to their teachers and peers will feel they have a significant place in their school community. To help foster academic achievement, parents or older students can alternate supervising tutoring or homework clubs before or after school. When they have a sense of accomplishment, students feel valued.

Talking to other parents and students at the school and visiting during classes are ways we can piece together a picture of what this place would be like for our child. Because a child's experience is an ongoing one, our evaluation of her school will change and grow. Throughout her school career, we have the right and the obligation to continue to assess how a child's school meets her needs. We were, after all, her first teachers and remain her most important advocates. No school is perfect, and no community can provide for every school's needs. There are many ways we can help. Each of them demands some commitment of time or energy, but the results can be priceless. Parents can join together to:

- meet regularly to discuss child- or school-related issues

- plan fund-raisers for enrichment materials and activities

- tap community resources as sponsors for special programs

In spite of their exposure to education as a series of individual disciplines to master, children naturally tend to see their world as a whole. As we know from experience, subjects are linked; talents and skills do not exist in isolation. Talent, when nurtured, easily overflows from one area to another. A school setting offers a child a chance to observe and interact with people of many talents and should promote and support the growth of each.

When schools provide opportunities for children to express their interests and talents, we recognize that each child is gifted in her own way.[20] It is our job as parents to help ensure that our children's strengths find a home after the bell rings.

TIPS TO TRY

A. Learning Environment
    School experiences should:
        develop communication skills and encourage
        individual talents.

B. Cooperative Learning
    Children:
        learn to interact socially, work in teams,
        and develop individual strengths.

C. Individual Learning
    Children:
        learn differently from each other, need positive adult
        reinforcement, and can work independently.

D. Outside Talents Inside School
    Motivation is the strongest ingredient in learning.
    Children learn best when they:
        are allowed to work at their own pace and like what
        they work on.

E. Special Gifts
    All children have special talents.
    Growth of talent is a continuous process.
    Children need a wide variety of enriching experiences.
    Parents should:
        keep teachers informed about the child, keep
        themselves informed about school, and find out how
        they can offer help.

F. Risk Taking and Creativity
    Creativity:
        comes from nonconformity, involves taking risks,
        leads to innovation and initiative, stimulates the
        excitement of learning, and can be contagious.

G. Evaluating Our Schools
    A school should:
        feel welcoming, encourage children to think, allow time
        to explore, present subjects from a variety of viewpoints,
        offer students a mixture of learning methods,
        appreciate students' special skills, encourage active
        learning, value the individual student, and encourage
        parental involvement.

10

Teamwork

SEVEN-YEAR-OLD Noreen was nervous. She was new on the swim team and did not know a soul. She went to the practices and worked hard. Soon she and two other girls began to seek each other out and sit together during down times. They traded charms and patches and admired each others' key chain ornaments. As her first meet approached, Noreen was anxious about competing. She sat with the team in the shade of their tarp as they played cards and joked to calm their jitters.

Noreen's first event was a graduated relay, and she was the youngest of five swimmers. The five stood together on the pool deck, the older ones with their arms around the younger ones' shoulders. "Don't think about anything but the water," said Katie, age twelve. "Just go in and do your best. I'll be at the other end cheering for you." Noreen did not win her heat, but she got lots of pats on the back when she finished. At the end-of-season team banquet, Noreen could hardly sit still; there were so many people she wanted to hug good-bye.

From the day our grubby seven-year-old marches into the kitchen with his friend in tow announcing, "Tommy is on a soccer team! Can I be on it, too?" we have entered another realm. As part of a team or group, a child becomes a member of a subculture based on interests, skills, or goals only achievable by joint effort. Some effort is required of parents as well.

In her early years, a child has a personalized setting. Her family treats her as an individual with her own way of reacting to the world. In preschool or play groups, she learns to deal with other children, one or two at a time. As a child begins the process of integrating her needs with those of her play or preschool companions, she learns to find her place within the group. She gravitates toward children and settings where she feels most comfortable. Interacting with her playmates, she begins to fill different roles as part of the group.

During her primary-grade years, she demonstrates her natural abilities, in the roles she adopts and the friendships she makes, as well as the activities she chooses. With these clues, parents can help her join more formal groups or teams. Slowly at first, with a child's consent (and perhaps enthusiasm), parents might locate a group or team for her to join with a friend, a comfortable way to begin a more demanding experience. A parent of a school or neighborhood friend might have ideas on where to start.

> Encourage a child to participate in activities where he can find *success*.

Often soccer teams, dance troupes, or choral groups are a good beginning. They provide groups built around minimal skill acquisition at the beginning levels and provide occasions to showcase the group to everyone's benefit. *Parents should beware of teams or groups that require advanced or developmentally inappropriate skills as a prerequisite for admission.* Even if a child has superior skills, the pressure of beginning at a level that emphasizes individual skills instead of a group focus can be extremely stressful to young children. They are often worried about achieving the *next* level and the shame of not measuring up. Orchestra participation and Little League baseball (requiring higher *individual* skill levels and more advanced eye-hand coordination than most primary grade students possess) are examples of groups more appropriate for later ages. When a child feels she belongs, she can blossom. A group functions best when its members are comfortable together.

A team or group has several members, with someone in the position of leader and usually an adult mentor or adviser. Most groups have a specific schedule of meeting or practice times and places, particular activities to accomplish, and rules by which to work; some have uniforms, costumes, or a dress code. From a scout group to a youth orchestra, from a wrestling team to volunteering for a political  campaign, *youngsters can find peers with similar interests in a group endeavor.* Adding additional transportation arrangements or yet another carpool, time commitments, and/or expenses for adults, why should a relatively sane parent permit his child to join a team?

Within a group a child can find:

- connectedness, a feeling of belonging

- uniqueness, a sense of himself as special

- empowerment, the capacity to be influential

- models who provide helpful examples of behavior or ideas[1]

Children are looking for a place to belong. In some communities children can still play driveway or playground basketball or a game of jacks on the sidewalk out front. But our adult schedules and concerns have increased our dependence on structured activities for our children, with the safety of adult supervision.

We can build on the desire for group involvement by helping children find settings that are welcoming and constructive. Gangs and cults might be welcoming, but they are far from constructive. In a supportive group setting, children are less likely to become involved in undesirable activities. They exercise, release energy and stress, and build self-esteem. Combining physical activity with friendships, team sports encourage physical and social development. When children compete in a supportive setting, they reach new limits.[2] As parents, we can encourage our child to participate in activities that promote success. Groups offer:

1. Membership

2. Positive relationships

3. Socialization

4. Skill development

5. Support from home

1. Membership

EACH OF US wants to belong. Even children who have difficulty in social group settings can benefit from groups based on skills or specific interests.[3] *When a child finds others with a similar focus, he is more likely to be socially comfortable.*

In contrast to the larger circles of school and community, children can find recognition within a team or group. Jim liked to build and fix things. Anything his family needed repaired was his domain. Individual projects appealed to

HOW KIDS MAKE THE MOST OF TEAM MEMBERSHIP

1. Join the group or team.
2. Wear the team "uniform".
3. Participate in team practices or rehearsals.
4. Arrive for group practices on time and stay for the duration.
5. Support team endeavors.
6. Undertake and complete satisfactorily tasks assigned as a group member.
7. Treat fellow team members as equally important.
8. Communicate with an appropriate team member (or adult) any issues of concern to resolve them in a positive way.
9. Extra credit! Take the initiative regarding activities or ideas beneficial to the team (bake sale, banners, prizes, rehearsal at home, etc.).

him more than high school clubs and teams. One day, he announced at dinner, "I'll probably be home late tomorrow; there's a tech meeting after school for the play." A couple of his friends had decided to get involved, and they invited Jim to come along.

The phone rang daily with calls for Jim from his friends on the lighting crew. They planned and replanned their strategy for the lighting requirements of each scene. Weekends were spent trying out their innovations. On opening night, Jim's parents looked around at all the technical equipment, expecting to find their son in a dark corner focusing a spotlight. Finally, they discovered him, at the top of a rig inches from the ceiling, running an entire band of lights and directing other members of the crew. He waved happily from his perch.

INTERGENERATIONAL GROUPS

Sometimes young people have opportunities to participate in activities with a different age group from their own. To satisfy her high school community service requirement, Gwen investigated all sorts of options. With some reservations, she tried out a group where students hosted senior citizens one morning a month. Participants from a nearby senior residence came by bus to Gwen's high school. When they arrived, they were greeted by an enthusiastic and welcoming group of students. They gathered together in a small classroom, where they discussed current affairs on each visit. The elderly people considered this program a refreshing highlight of their week. For the older citizens, the chance to share their time and interests with teens was a welcome change from their association with mostly elderly, often infirm, neighbors. For the high school group, it was interesting to learn different viewpoints from people who had been a part of history so much longer than they. One visit was all Gwen needed; she joined the group and remained an active participant long after she had satisfied her community service requirement.

A sense of belonging gives a child the security to be himself, to base his behaviors on his own personal convictions, rather than the dictates of others.[4] Members of gangs are not likely to have the self-esteem that enables them to think for themselves. The hallmark of a gang is conformity; the hallmark of a productive group is support and self-respect. Some schools and communities encourage youngsters to form clubs or groups by enabling students with similar interests and an adult teacher or sponsor to come together. The pride and pleasure of shared performances in music, dance and drama troupes, and sports teams are an added bonus.

Responsibility is important in group membership. Because of the interdependence of peers, youngsters learn how to give as well as receive. They recognize that they are responsible to the team just as they expect to be able to depend on their teammates. As in the old saying, "Ninety percent of life is showing up," ninty percent of group participation is being reliable. Six-year-old Kyle trembled. His first basketball game was coming up, and he was so anxious about it that he told his dad he could not go. "It's too scary," he whimpered. "I might not play well."

His dad sat down and perched Kyle on his lap. "I know you want to make every basket," he commiserated, "but no one does that, not even the pros. What we *do* expect, your mom and I and your teammates, is that you show up. You are part of a team, and your team is depending on you." With his high standards pushing him from within, Kyle became an asset to his team. No matter how tired he was, Kyle always showed up for his games.

However informal, every group has rules. Common expectations enable group members to work together. *Learning to create and abide by rules is an important social skill.* A group sometimes builds unity by adopting a name, a uniform, a logo, or a banner. Frequently, members who do not excel in the team's skill can offer such creative contributions.

Volunteer service work, religious group youth activities, and scout groups help develop empathy and enable young people to make a difference in the community. Group members also develop concern for the well-being of their teammates. They like and help each other; they want to succeed as a team.

One caution here: It is up to parents to set up rules that work for their family in terms of time and safety.

Sandy: *One spring, I allowed Andrew to play two sports simultaneously. He was on two soccer teams and a track team. Just finding ways for him to get to and from all the practices, in addition to allowing time for homework, was a struggle. Games and* *meets often conflicted with each other, and he was constantly torn between his choices. After such a stressful season, even Andrew agreed that he needed to limit his participation to one sport per season.*

Linda: *Cliff always wanted to play football, and Barry and I let him play on a local boys' club team when he was in middle school, where weight and age were regulated for safety. He won awards for his skill and sportsmanship and then wanted to play on the high school team. I refused to sign the permission forms, worried for the safety of this slim boy in competition with fellows of linebacker build. He was angry and disappointed but instead got involved in student government, the school newspaper staff, and all the musical and dramatic performances he could. He occasionally still reminds me that he thinks I should have let him play football, but I remind him of those other accomplishments that took football's place.*

2. Positive Relationships

MUTUAL SUPPORT IS a hallmark of a good team setting. When individual members give each other the encouragement to try, everyone benefits.

Sandy: *When Stephen entered high school, he joined the academic quiz bowl team, a group that competed locally and nationally in academic quiz meets. His dad and I were concerned about the pressure he would feel. "Don't worry," he breezily reassured us. "If you know the answer, you press the buzzer; if you don't, you don't!"*

By the end of the first season, his self-confidence had taken a nose-dive. The team lost an important match, and one of his blurted-out answers contributed to the defeat. When the team's adviser played back the video of their game, Stephen refused to watch. He had let his team down; he wondered whether he was qualified to be a member. His other teammates, all upperclassmen, commiserated; they reminded him of their own mistakes and the constant work it took to forge a team victory. During the summer, the team members met frequently to work on their skills and to go through mock quiz meets. When school began, Stephen was more optimistic. This time the team had a better season, and he was an asset to their efforts. As captain his senior year, he tried to give other team members the kind of support that had sustained him. The team had an undefeated year.

When children work together, they share in a task-related activity. In this setting, they exchange ideas, help each other, even teach each other, and learn teamwork. Cooperation evokes less stress, more creativity, stronger

> Real winners know the joy of the game is in its playing.

social skills, and greater problem-solving abilities. Team building includes respecting individual differences. Each child brings her own unique qualities to the group. In spite of their differences, children learn to support each other as members of the team. Whether they practice hockey, instrumental music, or academic tournament questions, youngsters discover that the whole team's performance improves through the continued group efforts. Several heads are better than one.[5]

The goal of peer relationships is cooperation among equals. The reciprocity that occurs in a child's peer group helps strengthen her self-image. Because a child usually feels more comfortable interacting with peers than with adults, she is more likely to continue her involvement and grow socially.[6] When children treat each other with kindness, they learn empathy more effectively than from any adult lecture. Peers can model kindness and generosity.

A child's self-image is bound up in his interactions with others. When a child builds positive relationships, he learns to feel good about himself.[7] In such a caring circle, when a child feels valued, he values others. While we teach children to like themselves, we also need to remind them that their talents do not make them superior, only special.

When a child misses a shot, strikes out, or fails in his own eyes, the security of our unconditional support is his best ally. Children become anxious about their performance when, for whatever reason, they feel incapable of producing the desired results. They want to please themselves, their parents, or their teammates—or all three. To inoculate children against the downward spiral of performance anxiety, we need to keep our expectations realistic.

Our attitude is our child's best protection against potential trouble. The pressure to excel can sometimes be overwhelming. Newspapers are full of stories about young people who have turned to dependence on harmful or illegal substances or dangerous behaviors. These and other self-destructive actions, such as fasting, binge-eating, or other eating disorders have no place in a healthy team environment. Many serious health risks result, and some undesirable effects are irreversible. Alert parents keep an eye out for changes in behavior that might signal problems and the need to seek help immediately.

A healthy sense of competition enables children to enjoy the excitement of team participation. When as participants or observers we keep our comments and our outlook positive, we model the kind of behavior we desire from our children. Kids learn from what they see. We should emphasize that real winners know the joy of the game is in its playing.

3. Socialization

A MICROCOSM OF society, a team provides the ground rules for socialization. *No matter how talented an individual is, his effectiveness depends on his ability to communicate with others.* Children learn this skill in relationships with their peers.

Sometimes involvement in a group can support development of social skills. In tenth grade, Joel was an outstanding student but not a very social fellow. He had an enormous amount of physical energy but had not quite hit on a way to channel it. He walked fast, he talked fast, and he thought fast, leaving other people constantly trying to catch up. People recognized his characteristic dash down the halls, books and papers tucked under his arms, the careless shirttail left out behind him.

One fall afternoon, there was a recruitment meeting of the yearbook staff. Although he had never worked on a yearbook before, Joel decided to try it out. He was assigned to the layout section, helping fit photographs and text aesthetically on each page. It was soon clear that he had a very good eye and a quick grasp of what was artistically appealing. More important, he went around the yearbook room helping the rest of the staff members arrange their stacks of photos and copy. The following year, he became layout chief and was an organizational whiz. His committee did its job with artistic flair and unusual promptness. Joel's quickness and enthusiasm energized his staff, as did his willingness to help others.

In his senior year, Joel was voted editor-in-chief by the entire staff. He managed the school's most comprehensive yearbook and brought it a coveted national high school journalism award. Several members of his staff became his lifelong friends.

Another important part of socialization is learning to resolve differences. Conflict resolution skills enable youngsters to compromise and appreciate each others' positions. Prosocial, assertive children more easily respond to another child's perspective and are more likely to initiate caring behavior. A *non*assertive child is more likely to help out only when she is *asked* to help.[8] When children listen to another's perspective, they can facilitate consensus. Participating in a group, they build the foundation for capable adult interactions.

Gender differences also appear in social interactions. Frequently, girls are more comfortable offering compassion and physical assistance; boys might rely on objects to lend or give.

A girl might hug a distraught teammate; her brother might provide a different bat or baseball glove.

Just having another group of friends can be reason enough to participate on a team. Drawing on a circle of youngsters from the larger community, a team offers an opportunity for more varied friendships.

Sandy: When Daniel was six, he joined the neighborhood soccer team. Energetic and physically active, he was a natural for the game. What was not natural for him was frequent, structured practices. After two years on the team, Daniel wanted out. I obliged but neglected to find him another sport or group activity. Though he seemed content with his school friends and his music lessons, he missed out on the enrichment of an organized group. When he formed a band in high school and spent four years on the drama department's sound crew, Daniel again felt the rewards of being part of a team.

Coaches and adult sponsors are models of behavior for the group. They teach teamwork, encourage group spirit, and motivate members to contribute their best.[9] Their philosophy of winning and losing drives the actions of their team. Children who direct epithets at opposing teams or argue with referees have not learned the principles of fair play. When a coach values each child's contribution and demonstrates it by positive words and actions, the group members have a clear model of supportive behavior to emulate. "Good try!" are two of the most important words a team member can hear.

> "Success, even in small doses, is the best preparation for the next step in learning."

4. Skill Development

ALTHOUGH IT IS beneficial for children to play for their own enjoyment, some youngsters relish developing their skills or acquiring new ones. Within a group, a child has three kinds of opportunities to improve his performance. First, in routine practice with teammates, he builds on his abilities. Second, if he is in the company of particularly skilled group members, he learns from their examples. Third, if he is especially talented, he can share his proficiency. He improves his own skills by teaching others. As Maria Montessori (founder of the Montessori schools) taught, a child's self-worth is connected with his sense of mastery of specific tasks. When a child chooses a new activity, he reaches for competence in a new area. Our support for this risk taking strengthens his confidence. "Success, even in small doses, is the best preparation for the next step in learning."[10]

When a child plays a sport, it is our responsibility as parents to be sure she has good equipment and a coach who stresses safety. Involvement of certified athletic trainers can help cut down on numbers and degrees of injuries.

With new mastery, a child reaffirms his self-worth.[11] Jerome, not really a team person, was happiest when he was off by himself, fishing. One day, he got a call from a friend. Some of his high school's families were starting a crew team, and they needed members. Would he consider joining? Jerome mulled it over. He loved to be near the water; being on it every day seemed pretty appealing. He had never rowed before, but how hard could it be? It was, after all, a brand new team, so there should be no overwhelming standards to meet, just an opportunity to try something that might be fun. He called back. "Okay, I'll try it," he said. "What do I have to do?"

A ten-year-old involved in an opera program for elementary school students was interviewed for a national television program. He was asked why he liked being in the group.

"When you're part of a team," he explained, "you're a part of something important."

—*Today Show*, NBC-TV, June 10, 1998

Within a few days, he and four other fellows, along with a women's team of eight girls, were meeting on the water every afternoon and getting acquainted with the basics of rowing. They practiced and exercised together, and they began to get in shape for their first season. Their parents, too, had to get in shape, but in a different way. They had to organize themselves so that all team members had transportation

to and from the water each day; in addition, they had to find numerous ways to raise funds for this fledgling team.

By the end of the season, a transformation had taken place: out of a disparate group of teenagers, from several grade levels, conflicting interests, and varied personalities, a team had formed. At the end-of-the-year potluck supper, all the team members huddled together. They would miss each other over the summer. They could not wait until practice would begin in the fall. And Jerome? He stood straighter; he smiled more often, his chest had filled out, and even his neck had grown thicker. His strong, broad shoulders and muscular arms testified to his hard work throughout the season. He had become an athlete; he was a rower and a proud member of the team.

Self-assurance, the realization that she *does* have something to offer her group, fuels a child's desire to belong. Someone who respects her own resources will seek opportunities to use them. Each child earns her own place in the group.[12] As parents, we must remember that skill acquisition progresses (often slowly) from the simple to the complex.

Patience is an important watchword for adults, as *persistence* is for children. Andrea's soccer team was losing. Worse still, they were close to ending the season without a single win. Now they were finishing the second game of their four-game tournament with—what else?—a loss. All the parents groaned at the thought of having another full day consumed with the last two tournament matches. "Couldn't we just concede?" one mother suggested. Several others agreed. Just the driving and waiting time was substantial enough, and the added expectation of two more losses seemed more than both players and parents should have to endure. "That's not what we want to teach them," one father quietly interjected. "They're not on this team to learn to give up when it's tough." Everyone nodded grimly. The next morning, the players piled into their cars, joking and playing cards all the way to the game; not one of them even mentioned the possibility of giving up.

Leaders are born through teams or groups. Sometimes children who do not excel in one area discover that their peers look to them for leadership in another. Frequently leaders of teams or interest groups are those with the best skill levels. Leadership qualities—good listening skills, awareness of creative alternatives, and negotiating ability—are sharpened in a group setting. The small size of a group or team affords a reticent child the opportunity to step up to a leadership role. "'I didn't set out to be a leader,'" mused one corporate vice president. "'I turned around and people were following me.'"[13]

A group setting might be just the place for a perceived deficiency to become an advantage. Tyler was small for his age. As his friends began growth spurts, first in elementary school, then in junior high school, he wondered whether he would ever be a normal size. His parents liked to be physically active, so at a young age, he had learned to play an

"My parents stressed learning how to win or lose; playing on a team is very important in any career. Boys and girls got equal treatment in my family."

—U.S. Senator Mary Landrieu (D-Louisiana), oldest of nine children, interview with authors, July 9, 1998 impressive game of tennis. He rode his bicycle, hung out with friends, and waited and waited for signs that he would grow.

When he entered high school, he noticed posters inviting new students to try out for the wrestling team. The only wrestling Tyler had ever done was tussling around on the floor with one of his brothers. Curious, he went to the weight room.

To his surprise, the coach was delighted to see him. "You're in just the weight class we need," he barked, slapping Tyler on the back. All around were strong and solid-looking fellows, none of whom was above average height. Then Tyler took a good look at the coach, a cheerful muscle-bound man. "He can't be over 5'4" tall," Tyler gasped to himself. He smiled back at the coach. "Sure," he grinned, "I'll give it a try."

After a high school career of winning strings of matches in his weight class, Tyler graduated as captain of the wrestling team. And when he walked to the podium at his new height of 5'6", he felt like the biggest guy in the room.

Problem-solving skills, often associated with leadership, can be strengthened in all group participants. Choosing a fundraising activity for the baseball team or a program for the orchestra recital involves negotiation. Youngsters who can negotiate a decision are improving their skill at solving problems.

Some children find that being a part of a group helps them get organized. To fit activities and schoolwork into their schedules, they must learn to manage their time. Through sports and performance demands, time management skills, attention, and concentration can all improve.

5. Support from Home

WHEN OUR CHILD is expected to succeed *on his own terms,* just as we expected him to learn to walk and talk, we give him the boost he needs for his efforts. *Every child is entitled to feel that his value to his family is not dependent on his accomplishments.* His motivation should be his alone, not what we impose. Failure occurs when he does not measure up to his own goals. Parents are responsible for helping children formulate goals that are realistic; we serve as guides in the process. We can review with our child what is necessary to accomplish his objectives. Does he need more practice for certain skills? Are some abilities more likely to increase as he gets older (certain kinds of fine-motor coordination, for example)? Would it help to have specific training? Perhaps going in a different direction altogether would be a good alternative.

> "**C**hildren who succeed in the game of life are children who fail but are encouraged to keep trying."

At times, adults need to intervene to help direct a child's choices. Nine-year-old Clint worked diligently practicing piano. At the end of his first year, the teacher called his parents. "I don't think Clint is having fun with his music," she said. "I really think he would enjoy a different instrument more." The next fall, he had a wonderful time learning his new instrument—trombone—with the school band.

Activities with others will be more appealing if children see parents involved in their own interest groups. Even if we have limited time and budget, we can make our homes welcoming places for adults and children. A child who observes her parents' participation in adult organizations might want to invite her own groups to her home.

As children explore different activities, parents can encourage developmentally appropriate choices. (Are they able to catch a small ball, or would kicking a soccer ball be more comfortable?) Is the environment one they will enjoy (is it too cold, too hot, too crowded)? If we push a child into an activity before he is ready, we invite disappointment and failure.

If we treasure our child for who he is, he can more easily withstand outside pressures for what he can do. It is a parent's job to recognize and communicate a child's uniqueness. An effective way to nourish potential is with consistent encouragement that targets particular strengths. When parents participate, whether by attending or assisting with transportation, preparing food, telephoning, or organizing, we communicate to our child that she deserves our time and energy. The support we offer by recognizing a child's abilities enables her to reach for further success. "Children who succeed in the game of life are children who fail but are encouraged to keep trying."[14] Parents provide encouragement by our investment of time, energy, and sometimes money for practice, play, coaching, training, equipment, special clothing, or entrance fees. Children thrive on the camaraderie of their teammates, but their most significant support begins at home.

An Added Bonus for Parents

IN COUNTLESS SOCCER, basketball, baseball, lacrosse, hockey, and swim teams and in endless dance, drama, and musical performing arts groups, parents unwittingly graduate when their children move on. We, too, are members of a team: the support team. The network we create gives us a different perspective on our children and their environment. As we focus on our children's interests, our adult teammates offer us their company, their understanding, and their store of information.

"You know," mused Mitch's mom to her friend, Lydia, "I'm really going to miss this group."

"It's true," Kerry's dad replied. "We're going to have to find a way to keep in touch." Seated in the prime center seats of the otherwise empty auditorium, the parents were preparing to take snapshots at the rehearsal of the high school choir's last performance of the year. For Kerry and Mitch, and seven other seniors in the group, this would be their final high school production. For their fathers and mothers, who had volunteered for numerous time-consuming jobs and driven countless miles to cheer at competitions and support performances no matter how far-flung their sites, this event marked the end of their official time together. Although grateful for

> "Some sports parents are road warriors who drive thousands of miles every season to help coach and provide the team snacks."
>
> —Maureen Harrington,
> "Families Driven to Keep Competitive in Sports," *USA Today*, April 27, 1998, p. 6D

release from their duties for the group, they realized that they, too, had formed a special bond.

Over cups of coffee in their kitchens and backstage through the years, the parents had agonized together about academic stress or discussed whatever current school issue was of concern. In their late-night meetings to plan who would host the concession tables or direct and produce the senior parents' show, they could discuss interesting summer programs. They even helped each other out by housing a son or daughter overnight if the adults were out of town. Through the years, they shared different views and experiences of their adolescents. In addition, they bolstered one another's confidence that their teens would weather the turbulence of adolescence successfully. They depended on each other. Supporting their children's efforts, they had helped bring out the strengths in one another. Graduation sure was going to be hard.

TIPS TO TRY

Encourage a child to participate in activities where he can find success.

A. In a group, a child can find:
      a sense of belonging, uniqueness, and leadership.

B. Membership can provide:
      social comfort, recognition, and responsibility.

C. Positive relationships can encourage:
      cooperation, empathy, realistic goals, and constructive activities.

D. Socialization can promote:
      communication skills, conflict resolution techniques, and positive role models.

E. Skill development includes:
      practice, learning from example, and teaching others.
    Adults need to have patience.
    Children need to have persistence.

F. Support from home should:
      be realistic in expectations, model group involvement, make home a welcoming place, and encourage appropriate choices.

11

A Family Affair

S HEILA WAS A child who always worried. Before
every birthday party she had a stomachache; before every new activity she was so nervous that she had to be forced
into going. When she was nine, her parents engineered a week's
stay with her grandparents, a treat just for her. After the first
two days of her visit, her anxious parents called. "Wish I could
talk now," Sheila said, "but I've really got too much to do.
See you soon!"

What had happened? Sheila had gotten to know her
grandmother and to observe a new approach to life. Her
grandmother, an outgoing, assertive person, could not pack
enough into her days. Art classes at a local college, sketching
trips, shopping, lunches out, visits to her grandmother's
friends, volunteering for charitable organizations, museum
jaunts, beach combing, movies, and cooking all spilled over
one upon the other into a kaleidoscope of exciting days for
Sheila. Everywhere they went, people seemed to know and
like her grandmother. Sheila decided that being a grandmother
must be the best thing anyone could do. Back home again,

Sheila's stomachaches began to decrease and her nervousness was balanced by her efforts to make new friends and engage in new experiences. She was beginning to see life less as a trauma and more as an adventure.

Often a child's best models are home-grown. Grandparents' interactions with their grandchildren can bring a gift no one else can duplicate, because they do it with love. As she grew, Sheila adopted her grandmother's perspective as her own; initiative, leadership, and innovation became her strengths. Her model had been a good one. "We can preach and lecture all we want, but to our children, our life really is our message."[1]

> "We can preach and lecture all we want, but to our children, our life really is our message."

How can the people closest to a child—his family—provide what he needs to develop his talents? Youngsters deserve a home with:

1. A responsive environment

2. Opportunities to learn

3. Models to emulate

4. Positive expectations

The "time, resources, and energy" family members provide enable a child to develop a sense of self-worth.[2] When children explore, question, and create in a caring environment, they can begin to develop their strengths. "Children's parents are the very best people to let them know that they are different, that there are no others in the whole world who are exactly like them, and that their differences are part of what makes them special and lovable."[3]

1. A Responsive Environment

WHEN WE THINK of tapping into the riches of our families to support a child's talents, we rarely think of transformations such as Sheila's. Stories like hers remind us that often our children's strengths are hidden and that a loving relationship could be all that is needed to uncover and nurture them. It can be a grandparent, aunt, uncle, cousin, or close family friend who brings this warmth to a child.

In a home where a child feels safe to share his ideas, work at his interests, and daydream, he will flourish. Nonjudgmental listening encourages trust. Time we can make available to them helps children develop autonomy. If we respect a child's need for time to pursue his interests, we invite his persistence.

Parents can "free [our] children to make efforts without concern for results."[4] Teaching children to handle failure and disappointment is as important as recognizing their achievements. Supportive parents understand that setbacks are inevitable. Unlike a school setting where a child's performance might be "scrutinized, judged, [and] weighed,"[5] at home a child should be free to wonder, to explore, to create, and to answer to his own standards. In contrast to doing his chores (necessary in every family), a child deserves the freedom of his own pursuits. A supportive parent "is a gift more valuable than tennis lessons . . . or a personal stereo."[6]

> "The opposite of courage in our society is not cowardice, it is conformity.'"

Divergent thinking, often less valued at school, is at a premium in a nurturing home. When we value creativity, youngsters know that problems can have many different solutions. Children like opportunities to offer their opinions; their views deserve respect. Family cohesiveness results from each member's expectation that his input is important. Families who brainstorm together view problems as opportunities; they point out connections, links, and parallels and encourage suggestions and ideas. They reinforce a youngster's individual perspective. Home is where a child should be able to try new approaches and take creative risks. "'The opposite of courage in our society is not cowardice, it is conformity.'"[7]

A true nonconformist, ten-year-old Henry would not wear shorts. Even on the warmest days, he insisted on long pants and shirts with collars. He carried his briefcase everywhere he went, along with his ever-present camera. While other kids played soccer, Henry made movies. Though his friends were not interested, his creations delighted his family. When he reached high school, he finally found another audience; he hosted and helped produce a lunchtime television talk show for his school. The support he received from his family enabled him to preserve his self-confidence until he was recognized and valued by his peers. When children experience our unconditional love, they learn that no achievement or failure affects their worth.

Of the gifts we give our children, our *time* is the most valued. *The myth of "quality time" may be comfortable to a busy parent, but "quality time" is inadequate for a needy child.* Frank Meyer, a public health professional, produced what he called "The Book of Time," a coupon booklet offering

Sandy: Jeff and I always look forward to Thanksgiving. Relatives from his side of the family come from around the country to spend the whole holiday weekend with us. From the strident screeches of greeting through the last lingering good-byes, the weekend is filled with noise and raucous laughter. The best part for the youngsters is that each one has always had a special family member he looks forward to seeing. All the younger cousins can't wait to greet 4'10" Aunt Pearl. When each child reaches her height, Aunt Pearl gives him a dollar. There are also several ongoing groups to plug into: the Scrabble group, the music makers, the discussion group, and the sightseers. There always seems to be a group of youngsters happy to play with each other and any adult who is willing. For that weekend, any disagreements or negative issues are consciously put aside; people enjoy just being in each others' company.

children pull-out receipts for "a walk . . . , a fishing trip, a tea party," and other activities to enjoy with a grown-up.[8] Time and attention are the growth ingredients that enable children to bloom. In a "resource-rich environment,"[9] people are as valuable as materials.

We are truly lucky if we have extended family to draw on. With effort on everyone's part, families can stay connected, no matter how far apart their members might be geographically. Holidays are natural gathering times, but other occasions (birthdays, graduations, a child's participation in a special program) lend themselves just as well to get-togethers. Regardless of the inevitable stress a variety of personalities tends to produce, we need to focus on the overall goal: the family unit is more important than individual disagreements. If some family members choose not to participate, that is their choice; we have to let them live with that decision and move on. One technique that encourages a positive outlook is to link each of our children with a relative who especially appreciates him. Then with each opportunity for a family event, the child looks forward to reconnecting with a favorite family member. This is a good  thing for adults to do for themselves as well. Families are worth the hard work it takes to keep them connected.

Families that live together also need time together. To counteract the many disruptions in our days, time with our nuclear family is important. Dinner or other family activities enable members to gather on a regular schedule. Research confirms that a child's attachment to her family is related to her participation in family occasions.[10] As families become geographically spread out, children miss out on multigenerational interactions. Knowing that adults are emotionally and physically available for her reinforces a child's self-esteem.

Linda: As a child, I dearly loved a very special doll. My grandmother loved to sew, and for this favorite doll, she produced an entire wardrobe of hand-smocked and ruffled creations. Whenever I played with Betsy Wetsy and these delightful clothes, I always thought of my grandmother. Many years later, those outfits, discolored and disintegrating, remain my treasures.

In less ideal situations, when a grandparent is in a nursing home, for example, visits from a grandchild can include bringing something to do or share. A photo album, a book, a school project, or a small pet visitor can all be welcome treats. Even a big envelope stuffed with news clippings, drawings, or other mementos of recent family doings is something an ill or elderly relative can look forward to when family members are far away.

2. Opportunities to Learn

AS PARENTS, WE need to set the stage for teachable occasions. Any member of a family can teach a skill, and those we love are often our best teachers. The motivation for learning to read, for example, is often social: the child is attached to the person who reads to her.[11] The grandfather who teaches his grandson to fish, or the aunt who introduces a special niece to the art of needlework, might seem like Norman Rockwell images in our minds, but with a little help, we can turn them into reality.

"Don't build walls; open doors."

A good teacher lets the child attempt her challenges without introducing his own accomplishments. When a child feels secure enough with her teacher to experiment, fail, and take risks to meet her goals, she has an environment that will encourage her talents. When a child's first experiences with a new skill are fun, he wants to continue. When his subsequent creations are acknowledged positively, he values his achievement. In a landmark study of highly successful adults, their parents, siblings, and relatives taught them informally when they were children, when interest was evident.[12] It seems an easy thing for experts to teach an eager child a skill. But even experts need to remember to *coach,* not to push, and to watch for the *child's* interest before setting a course of action. Effective teachers stimulate a child's interest, invite new approaches, and allow her development to evolve. "Don't build walls; open doors."[13]

How valuable is an adult teacher who is *not* an expert? The most important characteristic of a good teacher is concern for his student. With that commitment, anyone can become a teacher. Brady's mother was adamant that all three of her boys learn to swim. Beginning when they were toddlers, she took them to the local indoor pool three days a week for lessons. When Brady was old enough to join the group, the instructor moved away, and the pool management could not find a substitute.

"Why don't *you* do it?" the retiring instructor asked. Brady's mom protested that she was not an expert and had no training in teaching or in swimming. "You've been here for years," he reminded her, "and you know just what to do!" Reluctantly, she began a mini-career as a beginning swimming instructor. Brady, and lots of other toddlers, learned to swim beautifully, enjoying several years of lessons from his mother.

When we do not demand "instant correctness . . . and instead encourage children to do what they can," letting them know we are proud of their progress, we support their growing skills.[14] It does not take an expert to provide enthusiasm and encouragement. It *does* take someone whose attention is on the child.

An expert is needed when a child has reached a stage of proficiency requiring a high level of subject knowledge. Ginny was looking forward to her winter vacation. The family was going to the mountains, and her fondest dream was coming true: she was going to enjoy a whole week at her favorite sport—skiing. She would have a professional teach her every morning and then would go for practice runs in the afternoons with this same instructor. Ginny knew she was going to be terrific. Her ski instructor was her mom.

Sometimes things are not so ideal. Noelle wanted to learn to use her uncle's carpentry tools. He offered to help her learn by working with her and her friends to build a playhouse. But he was not as good a teacher as he was a builder. Uncomfortable letting the girls use the tools, he also could not bring himself to incorporate their ideas into his plans. As a result, the girls lost interest in the project; the playhouse sat ignored in the backyard. Disappointed, and at last realizing what he had done, Noelle's uncle tried a new tactic. He told his niece that his job was done and asked what improvements or changes she and her friends would suggest. Noelle jumped at this chance. With his help, she and her friends sawed another window in the back wall, built benches to sit on inside, and made a sign to hang over the door. Everyone was proud of the result, and Noelle was especially happy. She had learned to use the tools after all. Even a mistake can often be rectified when an adult tunes in to the child's needs.

"Personal choice is a powerful motivator for learning."[15] Children under age seven do not distinguish effort from ability. When they try something new, they believe they eventually will succeed. Between the ages of eight and twelve, they recognize that effort can compensate for talent. Adolescents are

"Wherever a teenager demonstrates a particular skill or interest, weave it into the fabric of your family life. . . . Ask your teenager to teach younger members of the family what he already knows. . . . This will . . . promote connectiveness in the family."

—Harris Clemes, Reynold Bean, and Aminah Clark,
How to Raise Teenagers' Self-Esteem
(Los Angeles: Price Stern Sloan, 1990), p. 61

more threatened by the prospect of falling short of their own or others' standards. Sometimes peers or understanding adults can persuade a reluctant teen to take a creative risk. Overwhelmed by too much adult help, a child loses confidence.

Providing just enough guidance for a child to extend his efforts toward further growth is sometimes referred to as "scaffolding."[16] Reasoning, information gathering, alternative strategizing, and evaluation of possible outcomes are effective skills in solving real-life problems. They are the foundations of a scaffolding relationship. Time is essential in fostering these skills; so are mentoring parents. No talent blossoms in isolation. Every child deserves the backing of her family.

The brother and sister of an academically gifted youngster (whose immigrant parents had only completed fifth grade) took it upon themselves to encourage his success. From her small salary, his sister bought him a new book every payday. His brother, studying medicine, pushed him to excel. "He believed that if he gave me enough stimulation, something would excite me, something would click. He was right."[17] This young boy grew up to become one of the world's leading surgeons and cancer researchers: Dr. Steven Rosenberg.

> "The best thing you can give to anyone is what you do best."

"Creativity brings people together."[18] Endeavors that stimulate imaginative or artistic responses invite our participation with children. Hobbies can be enjoyed together. Whether parent or child initiates an interest, both can derive satisfaction from sharing their information and enthusiasm. Even if a child's interests are not shared by a parent, the support for her efforts is important. Children find their talents through hobbies.

A child can benefit from having a mentor, other than a parent, involved in helping explore a chosen subject. The relationship that a different family member (or close family friend) already has with a child can make mentoring extremely positive. The significant contribution of a mentor

is her commitment and concern for the child. In a supportive extended family, frequently a member one or two
generations older is a good choice. As a family's "emotional
leaders," grandparents may have the stature to assume a
mentoring role.[19] They often have a "magic ingredient" that
busy "parents do not: time."[20] While teaching skills, they
might also inadvertently teach ethics, morals, and behavior.[21]
Whether it is in the park, a workroom, or the kitchen, a grandparent can be a "master teacher."[22]

Because a grandparent's love and acceptance are not usually contingent
upon achievement, a child thrives with
such a special mentor. Frank loved to
play baseball. Every chance he got, he
was in the backyard practicing his pitch
against the wall of the garage and throwing balls into the air to hit into the
bushes. When he was old enough, he
joined a team. His father, who had enjoyed baseball as a youngster, became the
coach. But the highlight of Frank's weekend was when Grandpa arrived. He donned his old cap,
grabbed a well-worn glove, and took over the park's ballfield
with his grandson. Together they worked on hitting and field-
ing techniques, unraveled the mysteries of fast balls and sliders,
and anticipated strategies from the bench. Frank was lucky.
His devoted grandpa had played baseball in the minor leagues.
"The best thing you can give to anyone is what you do best."[23]
Some older people do not have grandchildren or do not have
any living nearby; they might welcome being "adopted" into
a family in need of grandparenting. People of all ages have
talents to share.

Families have different ways of sharing information. One
family treats the children to stories about their relatives and
the special talents remembered in each. While youngsters can
inherit their family members' looks, there might be an extra
added dividend: they might also inherit their abilities.

Grandparents provide "the link between the past and the present, and are perhaps the best interpreters of the significance of time in our lives."

—James Alvino and the editors of *Gifted Children Monthly: Parents' Guide to Raising a Gifted Child* (New York: Ballantine, 1985), p. 39

Linda: When family members share an interest, they can teach each other. Barry is a business executive. He loves the strategies of the wholesale and retail marketplaces and the excitement of trying to outmaneuver others in his field. At a young age, our son Aaron learned about stocks and soon began his own little investment portfolio. He and Barry would check the stock pages daily to discuss the day's business climate and evaluate Aaron's earnings. He began to ask Barry lots of questions about the family business. By the time he went to college, Aaron was considering business as a possible career choice. He had already been given some basic training.

In addition to what comes naturally, children learn by example. Elsa grew up in an apartment above her father's tailor shop. After school, she spent hours watching him painstakingly hand-finish garments for his customers. He was known for his meticulous work and his attention to detail. Elsa watched and learned. Through her father's example, she learned that with patience and care, she could also produce beautiful handwork. Her exceptional needlepoint and crewel creations now adorn all her children's homes.

Extended family can also be a resource. "I have a question," twelve-year-old Doug would begin. Ever since he was very young, Doug loved a discussion. Nearly any topic stimulated his curiosity and provoked opinions. His penchant for debate earned him a family nickname: "the attorney." As he grew, his interests spanned world events, political issues, and ethical concerns. Whenever he wanted to engage in a lengthy, legalistic analysis, there was one person who always had time to talk and listen—his grandfather. Fortunately for Doug, his grandfather was retired; equally fortunate was his profession: he was a lawyer.

3. Models to Emulate

MARSHALL ALWAYS ADMIRED Uncle Saul. He was an entrepreneur, constantly incubating ideas to write about or pursue as different facets of his career. The family joke was that as soon as Uncle Saul completed a job, he would just invent another one and begin anew. Marshall's parents wanted him to have a law degree, like his father, but Marshall always wanted to be like Uncle Saul. He compromised by getting his law degree first and then setting out to run his own consulting group. With his fingers in lots of pies, he was just like Uncle Saul.

Being a model of divergent thinking and creativity, like Marshall's Uncle Saul, is a special gift. It encourages a child to be brave and self-reliant and to find his strengths within himself. People who are most content as adults value themselves.

Children enjoy emulating others, especially those they love. As teenagers, young people cite family members as the people they most admire. As models, people who exemplify desired characteristics, family members can have a particularly strong impact on children. Every Friday afternoon, Ben, a business owner, and his elderly mother volunteer at the senior center. He conducts a religious service and leads a lively discussion. The members all love to participate. Though Ben's grown children live away from home, they know their father's Friday

> "Parents have to be role models. They have to live by what they say, in order to build trust in a child."
>
> —Esther B. Heller,
> guidance counselor, interview with authors, July 9, 1998

"My Aunt Sophie was the only family member interested in the arts. She was the one who took me to the theater, to art galleries, and to concerts. . . . Expose children to new experiences; give them every opportunity you can!"

—Aline Gross Sayer,
assistant professor of human development, Penn State University,
interview with authors, July 5, 1998

afternoon commitment, and they join him when they are in town. Never a lecturer on charity or morality, Ben has modeled his beliefs, and his children have absorbed the lesson. Children learn more from observing others than from advice.[24]

A child may find in a family member an interest that has special appeal. She may look to that person as an example of how to pursue it. Many famous performers in the arts and sports have followed in a loved one's footsteps. Sometimes a child will consider a relative's talent as permission to challenge herself in that field.

Four-year-old Judith desperately wanted to be able to do cartwheels like her six-year-old brother, Herb. She watched his effortless gymnastics and tried and tried and tried to imitate them. One day when her Aunt Lila was visiting, Judith pulled her over to see her perform. "Watch me! Watch me!" Judith squealed, as she executed one perfect cartwheel after another. Her surprised aunt asked how she had learned so well. "Oh, I copied Herb," Judith proudly declared. "He teached me!"

Marian Wright Edelman, founder of the Children's Defense Fund, grew up in a home where "service [was] the rent . . . for living . . . not something you do in your spare time."[25] When there was a need in the community, her parents led the way to resolving it. When black children were not allowed on public playgrounds, her father built one behind the church. Because no old-age facilities accepted African Americans, her parents founded and ran one across the street from their home. When she was later asked what she did as a profession, Edelman realized, "I do exactly what my parents did, just on a different scale."[26]

Any family member can be the available, interested person in a child's life. Aunt Josie's was a favorite place for Drew and his brothers to visit. A talented amateur musician, she was always interested in their music. No matter what the instrument or musical style, she was an attentive and knowledgeable audience. Sometimes she had interesting music to share; other times she just shared herself.

Sandy: At five, Andrew loved words. He liked their sounds; he liked to play with their meanings. He bought books of word games, puns, and riddles. He loved to write. One summer, Jeff

and I took a week-long trip, and Stephen (then twenty and a college English major) stayed with him. When we returned, Stephen felt compelled to offer some advice. Because of Andrew's interests, he announced, we should expose him to better literature. Poetry was an obvious choice for Stephen; his young charge loved stories of warfare, so Stephen had been reading nightly from The Iliad. *Jeff and I looked at each other; providing proper enrichment would be a challenge!*

4. Positive Expectations

A FAMILY WITH positive expectations of their children does not necessarily promote Olympic athletes, concert pianists, or Nobel Prize winners. It *does* expect children to succeed according to their own standards and has patience to let its children develop their skills at their own paces. In a home where we provide time, attention, and love, our children are motivated to pursue their own passions. For children to grow in their accomplishments, they need adults who will listen. When we transmit our own positive perspective, our children develop a similar outlook. Youngsters who are optimistic are "happier, more successful, . . . and actually physically healthier."[27] A positive worldview encourages children to focus on solutions rather than on problems and boosts their self-confidence.[28] "Your family is different," Terry remarked to Sasha on her first visit with Sasha's family. "You're all *expected* to do your best." Our "children develop an optimistic attitude by watching and listening" to us.[29]

In a family with siblings, a younger child can have a special burden. She might see an older brother rewarded for a level of talent she wishes she, too, could achieve. Accentuating their different kinds of abilities frees each from comparison with the others. Larry was always exceptional. By the time he was eight years old, he was choosing his father's medical books for his bedtime reading. In high school, his English teacher said he was one of the best writers she had taught. As a freshman in college, he taught computer classes to older students. He had only one problem: he was so disorganized that with the exception of his computer assignments, his work was often lost or incomplete. The high-tech company that hired him while he was still in college, however, did not care.

"I remain totally convinced that, to get off to the best start in life, what new humans need is a great deal of waking time . . . with older people who are deeply in love with them."

—Burton L. White, Ph.D.,
The First Three Years of Life (Upper Saddle River, NJ: Prentice Hall, 1985), p. 328

Larry's younger brother, Marv, also an excellent student, was an expert at organization. In high school, he founded and ran an investment club, to teach other students about the stock market. Personable and quietly assertive, at seventeen he networked his way around Congress while working as a summer intern. "I just wanted to meet interesting people," he told his parents, who were amazed at his self-promotion, "and at those parties, the food was really good!" Encouraged in their different strengths from a very young age, these boys participated in activities of their own choosing, from a computer mentoring program for Larry to a *Wall Street Journal* subscription for Marv. Their parents enjoyed the different successes of each child.

In many cases, a particular talent runs in the family. A younger sibling might be as capable as an older one but not yet be old enough for his ability to have matured. Often a parent can help a child find in the *same* subject area a focus different from his sibling's and a different mentor or activity to pursue it. An obvious caution for parents is to avoid comparisons. Our nonjudgmental acceptance of each child reminds him of his uniqueness. A child's resentment and frustration are natural; parents can be effective sounding boards for these feelings.

Able siblings can work together on projects that enhance the contribution of each. Del, thirteen, and his older brother, Shane, were both musical. Shane, at sixteen, was a serious pianist who won local competitions. He was acknowledged in the family as a talented musician. Del had taken violin lessons, but by age eleven, he wanted to play piano as well. He, too, was talented, but his parents were wary of sibling competition. A teacher suggested that Del might enjoy studying music composition; Del was a natural. Composing music was a focus for his exceptional creativity and sensitive ear. He began to win recognition for his work.

For a special recital, Del needed a pianist who could perform his latest composition, a particularly complex piece. He chose his older brother. After the performance, amid the applause, Del's brother rose and beckoned to Del to stand and take credit for his work. Their parents were not the only ones in that audience with tears in their eyes.

Like childhood, parenting time is fleeting. We give of ourselves; we respect our children as individuals. When each child is ready, we prepare to let go, confident that he will find his own special way of going through life. We have only a short span of years to help our children realize their potential. They grow up and move on. Each child needs to feel he is important in *our* lives as the basis for his importance in his own. The value we place on our jobs as parents and as mentors reveals our priorities—to our children, to ourselves, and, as a result, to the world around us.

TIPS TO TRY

Family members can help a child develop his talents.

A. A Responsive Environment
    Children need a setting that:
    encourages trust, stimulates creative thinking,
    offers unconditional love, and brings family members
    together to share their time.

B. Opportunities to Learn
    Children learn by:
    taking risks, being coached, solving problems,
    reasoning, and sharing interests and activities
    with others.
    Children are encouraged by:
    family members, friends, mentors, and models/
    examples.

C. Models to Emulate
    Children like:
    having role models and developing new interests by
    learning from other family members.

D. Positive Expectations
    Positive expectations encourage children to try new things.
    Acceptance of each child's abilities without judging her
    shows appreciation for her as a person.

12

NOW WHAT?

Now that we know what they like, where can we take our children for stimulation and fun? How can we find what resources are available to us, and how can we access them?

We discovered many opportunities for families. Especially for moms working outside the home, *Working Mother* (www.workingmother.com) has for years helped deal with the juggling act this kind of schedule involves. Other helpful Internet sites are:

www.women.com is a place where career experts share advice and stories about career and family issues women face.

www.aboutwork.com deals with self-employment and how to integrate employment issues with family ones.

And there is an organization especially for single moms, helpful for single dads as well:

The National Organization of Single Mothers, Inc.
P.O. Box 68
Midland, NC 28107-0068
(704) 888-KIDS

For single dads, especially:

National Fatherhood Initiative
One Bank Street, Suite 160
Gaithersburg, MD 20878
(301) 948-0599

As we look around us, are there woods, streams, ponds, mountains, fields, or farms nearby? What can we see and do in these places? Outdoors or indoors, children are interested in how their world works. A good source for science information is:

Science-by-Mail (kits for fourth to ninth graders)
Museum of Science
Science Park
Boston, MA 02114
(800) 729-3300
www.mos.org

Where are there hiking or biking trails? Is there somewhere we can learn to fish, or ride a horse? Camping, too, can be a wonderful experience for kids with or without their families; helpful information is available through:

American Camping Association, Inc.
5000 State Road 67 North
Martinsville, IN 46151-7902
(765) 342-8456
www.aca-camps.org

Where is the nearest library? Is there a children's room? Even better, is there a children's library in our community or in one nearby? What kinds of programs do our libraries offer for children and for what ages? We want to be on their mailing lists. Do they have any parenting programs? Other parents make wonderful resources and friends.

Where are the nearest museums, and what can we find out about them? What resources and programs do they have for children? Some local newspapers offer a weekly or monthly list detailing special activities and exhibits. This is a good page to tear out and post at home.

Are there any art galleries nearby? Sometimes the small two- or three-room variety is the best kind for early exposure to works of art. And we want to be sure to include abstract art, so our children can be aware of a variety of approaches.

Does our community, or a neighboring one, have recreation or nature centers? Can we get on their mailing lists? We might try out some of the parent-child activities. Is there a wildlife refuge in our area? We can visit with our child and perhaps volunteer to help in some way. For more information, we can contact:

Audubon Society, Education Department
700 Broadway
New York, NY 10003
(212) 979-3000

The Wilderness Society
900 17th Street, NW
Washington, DC 20006-2596
(202) 833-2300

Where are our local playgrounds? If we go regularly to the same one, we will meet other kids and their families eventually, which can make going to the playground a special social event.

Do we have a roller-skating rink in the area? Ice skating? When are lessons offered and for what ages? When is "free skate" time, for families to enjoy together?

What programs do our local bookstores offer? Can we get on their mailing lists, too? After all, they want to sell us books for and about our children. In many cases, they also offer story times and helpful talks. Some areas have bookstores devoted only to children's books. Some magazines are specifically for children; others invite children's contributions as well:

Cobblestone: The History Magazine for Young People
7 School Street
Peterborough, NH 03458
(603) 924-7209

***Cricket* Magazine Group**
315 5th Street
Peru, IL 61354
(815) 224-6656
(800) 588-8585

Ebony Jr!
820 S. Michigan Avenue
Chicago, IL 60605
(312) 322-9200

Highlights for Children (ages two to twelve)
803 Church Street
Honesdale, PA 18431
(800) 255-9517

Sesame Street Magazine
P.O. Box 5200
Boulder, CO 80322-2000
(800) 840-9392

Stone Soup: The Magazine by Children
Box 83
Santa Cruz, CA 95063
(408) 426-5557
www.stonesoup.com

National Written and Illustrated by Children Awards
Landmark Editions
Box 4469
Kansas City, MO 64127
(816) 241-4919
www.landmarkeditions.com

What historical landmarks are in our area? Are there battle-fields, monuments, or other historic sites? Is there a local historic or preservation association? What kinds of programs do they provide? Are there any walking tours, hikes, or boat rides?

We can visit local winter sport supply stores and find stacks of free brochures with details of the many places to go skating, snowshoeing, skiing, snowmobiling, and winter hiking. We want to find information on lessons for beginners. Can we participate in any free introductory programs?

What kinds of people are accessible at their work in our community? The grocers, pharmacists, store owners, firefighters, police officers, nurses, doctors and hospital administrators, mail carriers, gas station managers, and local government figures might be able to set up times for us to visit and tour and ask questions about their work and their workplaces.

How can we find the craftspeople in our community? We can watch and talk with artists who paint, sculpt, sketch, weld, or weave. We can attend a crafts show, where we can talk with the craftspeople and watch some of them at work. Crafts supply stores often offer classes; maybe we can learn to make our own crafts. The local 4-H classes run the gamut from photography to fly tying.

What other kinds of fairs are there? Does our community have county fairs or harvest festivals? What a great place to see lots of animals! There might be amusement rides, roping competitions, and pumpkin-judging contests. Schools often have fairs; preschoolers will love the nursery school carnivals geared just for their age group.

Theater performances are wonderful options to investigate. High school shows are perfect for introducing children to theater. School musicals, vocal and instrumental concerts, and plays all offer glimpses into areas our children might like to try out for themselves. Such programs are convenient and inexpensive (or even free) and very much appreciated by the children who can see other children doing marvelous things.

Children are accustomed to watching videos on their home televisions. But going to a real movie theater is exciting. When a child is old enough, foreign films can open a window on other cultures. Kids old enough to read comfortably might enjoy reading plays. Screenplays can be stimulating for technically oriented youngsters.

School sporting events are fun to watch, and children can learn about various sports as spectators even before they are developmentally able to participate. Again, sponsored by schools, these are close by and free or inexpensive.

Churches, synagogues, and other organizations offer carnivals and family programs and films; where are they listed in our neighborhood? Maybe there is a bulletin board at the grocery store, in the YMCA, or at the library. The local newspaper often provides details. Circling interesting possibilities will make them easy to spot when we look for them later.

What about the media? Can we visit our newspaper's office and take a tour? Can we tour the television and/or radio stations? Maybe we can sit in an audience for a show!

Are grandparents or aunts and uncles nearby? When can we visit? Intergenerational experiences are valuable and fun. We can also share someone else's grandparents if our children's are far away. Many senior residences and nursing homes have adopt-a-grandparent programs.

Older people welcome the exuberance of youth, and our children can enjoy the attention of elderly adults.

When children give of their own time and resources, they learn to value the needs of others. What organizations exist in our community to help other people? How can our family volunteer to help? Even a very young child could add the napkins to boxes of food being prepared for distribution to homeless people or help deliver toiletries or clothing to a shelter. Is there a retirement building, a nursing home, or a hospital that would welcome our offer to help? Maybe our children would like to perform for such groups or for adult day-care programs. Do our kids like to sing or play an instrument or recite poetry or monologues? Do they like to make up skits and act them out? We can share what they like to do with others who would appreciate their efforts and energy. Even a new reader could entertain a person who is house-bound. It would provide the reader with a chance to practice and the listener with needed companionship. Some ideas for volunteer opportunities include:

American Red Cross, Youth Associates Program
National Office of Volunteers
431 18th Street, NW
Washington, DC 20006
(202) 737-8300
www.redcross.org

American Society for the Prevention of Cruelty to Animals
441 E. 92nd Street
New York, NY 10128
(212) 876-7700

Environmental Defense Fund
Public Information Department
New York City
(800) 684-3322
www.edf.org

The Lighthouse, Inc. (for the blind)
Information and Resources
(800) 334-5947

Literacy Volunteers of America
(315) 472-0001
www.literacyvolunteers.org

People for the Ethical Treatment of Animals
501 Front Street
Norfolk, VA 23510
(757) 622-7382

Embassies and consulates are valuable sources of information on foreign cultures. There are international programs for children to participate in and opportunities to study the languages and cultures of other countries. One interesting center for language study is:

Concordia College
Concordia Language Villages
Moorhead, MN
(800) 222-4750

Teachers often learn as much as their students. What is our child good at? Maybe she could teach someone else who would like to learn that skill. Maybe she could be useful, for example, to someone else who is not yet at ease using a computer.

For outside mentors or adult helpers, we can try:

MENTOR: The National Mentoring Partnership
1400 I Street, NW, Suite 850
Washington, DC 20005
(202) 729-4345
FAX: (202) 729-4341
www.mentoring.org

Big Brothers Big Sisters of America
National Office
230 N. 13th Street
Philadelphia, PA 19107-1538
(215) 567-7000
www.bbbsa.org
E-mail: bbbsa@aol.com

Organizations such as the American Automobile Association offer (for their members) a wealth of brochures, booklets, and maps about the locations, hours, and phone numbers of local museums, sites of interest, and activities. This material is a wonderful source of ideas for a variety of ages.

American Automobile Association
1000 AAA Drive
Heathrow, FL 32746-5063
(Check phone book for a local office.)

Some Reminders

- *Call* for information; hours, directions, and fees might have changed.

- Take along maps and brochures.

- Share plans with the family; children like to know what to expect.

- Pack with contingencies in mind—sunscreen, umbrella, water bottles. Day or fanny packs children can carry themselves are helpful for day-long and outdoor excursions.

- Review safety and consideration rules.

- Take a camera, sketchbooks, pencils, and containers for collectibles.

- Be prepared. An astonishing result can occur: after years of being coaxed to go to nature centers, art galleries, museums, and other centers of culture, when the kids grow up, they go on their own!

NOTES

Chapter Two

1. Linda Eyre and Richard Eyre, *Teaching Children Joy* (New York: Ballantine, 1984), p. 152.

2. T. Berry Brazelton, pediatrician, interview with authors, January 15, 1999.

3. Cheri Fuller, *Unlocking Your Child's Learning Potential* (Colorado Springs: Navpress, 1994), p. 128.

4. Burton L. White, *The First Three Years of Life* (Upper Saddle River, NJ: Prentice Hall, 1985), p. 297.

Chapter Three

1. T. Berry Brazelton, *Toddlers and Parents: A Declaration of Independence* (New York: Dell, 1974), p. x.

2. Brazelton, p. xi.

3. RaeLynne P. Rein and Rachel Rein, *How to Develop Your Child's Gifts and Talents during the Elementary Years* (Los Angeles: Lowell House, 1994), p. 11.

4. Dorothy Corkille Briggs, *Your Child's Self-Esteem* (Garden City, NY: Doubleday, 1975), p. 282.

5. Briggs, p. 281.

6. Cited in Bernard S. Raskas, *Heart of Wisdom* (New York: Burning Bush, 1962), p. 115.

7. T. Berry Brazelton, *Infants and Mothers* (New York: Dell, 1969), p. 281.

Chapter Four

1. Felton Earl and Mary Carlson, "Towards Sustainable Development for American Families," *Daedalus* 122, no. 1 (Winter 1993): 107.

2. Kenny Luck, *52 Ways to Nurture Your Child's Natural Abilities* (Nashville: Nelson, 1994), p. 46.

3. Thomas Armstrong, *Awakening Your Child's Natural Genius: Enhancing Curiosity, Creativity, and Learning Ability* (New York: Putnam's, 1991), p. 56.

4. James M. Harris, *You and Your Child's Self-Esteem* (New York: Warner, 1989), pp. 85.

5. Isabelle Fox, *Being There* (New York: Barron's, 1996), p. 130.

6. Benjamin S. Bloom, *Developing Talent in Young People* (New York: Ballantine, 1985), p. 471.

7. Harris, pp. 79-80.

8. Armstrong, p. 23.

9. Joan Franklin Smutny, Kathleen Veenker, and Stephen Veenker, *Your Gifted Child: How to Recognize and Develop the Special Talents in Your Child from Birth to Age Seven* (New York: Ballantine , 1989), p. 19.

10. Armstrong, p. 8.

11. Wayne W. Dyer, *What Do You Really Want for Your Children?* (New York: Avon, 1985), p. 47.

12. Richard Carlson, *Celebrate Your Child: The Art of Happy Parenting* (San Rafael: New World Library, 1992), p. 59.

13. Carlson, p. 79.

14. Carl Addison Takacs, *Enjoy Your Gifted Child* (Syracuse, NY: Syracuse University Press, 1986), p. 118.

15. Dyer, p. 375.

16. Armstrong, p. 56.

17. Smutny, Veenker, and Veenker, p. 23.

18. Smutny, Veenker, and Veenker, p. 15.

19. James Alvino and the editors of *Gifted Children Monthly, Parents' Guide to Raising a Gifted Child* (New York: Ballantine, 1985), p. 141.

20. Foster Cline and Jim Fay, *Parenting with Love and Logic* (Colorado Springs: Pinon, 1990), p. 26.

Chapter Five

1. Thomas Armstrong, *Awakening Your Child's Natural Genius: Enhancing Curiosity, Creativity, and Learning Ability* (New York: Putnam's, 1991), p. 126.

2. Richard Carlson, *Celebrate Your Child: The Art of Happy Parenting* (San Rafael: New World Library, 1992), p. 86.

3. Carlson, p. 25.

4. James Alvino and the editors of *Gifted Children Monthly, Parents' Guide to Raising a Gifted Child* (New York: Ballantine, 1985), p. 141.

5. Carlson, p. 92.

6. Carlson, p. 87.

7. Ruth M. Cass, artist, interview with authors, June 2, 1998.

8. Jane M. Healy, *Your Child's Growing Mind* (New York: Doubleday, 1994), p. 325.

9. Neil Baldwin, *Edison: Inventing the Century* (New York: Hyperion, 1995), pp. 18–19.

10. RaeLynne P. Rein and Rachel Rein, *How to Develop Your Child's Gifts and Talents during the Elementary Years* (Los Angeles: Lowell House, 1994), p. 51.

11. Fred Rogers and Barry Head, *Mr. Rogers Talks with Parents* (Pittsburgh: Family Communications, 1983), p. 132.

12. Karl Erb, "Solitude," *Brandywine: Georgetown Day High School Literary Magazine* (Washington, D.C.).

13. Rogers and Head, p. 135.

14. Carlson, p. 89.

15. Armstrong, p. 126.

16. Healy, p. 325.

17. Jane Piirto, *Understanding Those Who Create* (Dayton, OH: Psychology Press, 1992), p. 50.

18. Piirto, p. 49.

19. Benjamin S. Bloom, *Developing Talent in Young People* (New York: Ballantine, 1985), p. 468.

20. Carlson, p. 29.

21. Piirto, p. 50.

22. Rhoda Kellogg and Scott O'Dell, *The Psychology of Children's Art* (New York: CRM–Random House, 1967), p. 17.

Chapter Six

1. Mary Leonard, "As More Children Are Overbooked, Play Gives Way to Achievement," *Boston Globe*, April 19, 1998, p. G2.

2. Jane M. Healy, *Your Child's Growing Mind* (New York: Doubleday, 1994), p. 320.

3. Healy, p. 321.

4. Healy, p. 320.

5. Bamberger, cited in Jane Piirto, *Understanding Those Who Create* (Dayton: Ohio Psychology Press, 1992), p. 304.

6. Healy, pp. 317–318.

7. Healy, p. 318.

8. Benjamin S. Bloom, *Developing Talent in Young People* (New York: Ballantine, 1985), p. 518.

9. Jane Piirto, *Understanding Those Who Create* (Dayton, OH: Psychology Press, 1992), p. 304.

10. Donna B. Gray, *A Parent's Guide to Teaching Art* (White Hall, VA: Betterway, 1991), p. 20.

11. Gray, p. 21.

12. James Alvino and the editors of *Gifted Children Monthly, Parents' Guide to Raising a Gifted Child* (New York: Ballantine, 1985), p. 183.

13. E. Paul Torrance, *Guiding Creative Talent* (Upper Saddle River, NJ: Prentice Hall, 1962), p. 171.

14. Piirto, p. 303.

15. Cheri Fuller, *Unlocking Your Child's Learning Potential* (Colorado Springs: Navpress, 1994), p. 128.

16. Bloom, p. 459.

17. Joan Franklin Smutny, Kathleen Veenker, and Stephen Veenker, *Your Gifted Child: How to Recognize and Develop the Special Talents in Your Child from Birth to Age Seven* (New York: Ballantine, 1989), p. 161.

18. Fuller, p. 176.

19. David Elkind, *The Hurried Child* (Reading, MA: Addison-Wesley, 1988), p. 171.

20. Healy, p. 323.

21. Elkind, p. 9.

Chapter Seven

1. Patricia Marks Greenfield, *Mind and Media: The Effects of Television, Video Games, and Computers* (Cambridge, MA: Harvard University Press, 1984), p. 128.

2. Faith Clark and Cecil Clark, *Hassle-Free Homework* (New York: Doubleday, 1989), p. 210.

3. Thomas Armstrong, *Awakening Your Child's Natural Genius: Enhancing Curiosity, Creativity, and Learning Ability* (New York: Putnam's, 1991), p. 172.

4. Joan Anderson and Robin Wilkins, *Getting Unplugged: Take Control of Your Family's Television, Video Game, and Computer Habits* (New York: Wiley, 1998), p. 67.

5. James Alvino and the editors of *Gifted Children Monthly, Parents' Guide to Raising a Gifted Child* (New York: Ballantine, 1985), p. 329.

6. Sharon A. Edwards and Robert W. Maloy, *Kids Have All the Write Stuff: Inspiring Your Children to Put Pencil to Paper* (New York: Penguin, 1992), p. 200.

7. Greenfield, p. 134.

8. Jane M. Healy, *Your Child's Growing Mind* (New York: Doubleday, 1994), p. 26.

9. Karen Rosenbaum, "Kids and Computers," *Parents' Perspective* radio program, September 10, 1997.

10. Greenfield, p. 110.

11. Greenfield, p. 103.

12. Greenfield, pp. 113, 115.

13. Edwards, p. 193.

14. Edwards, p. 192.

15. Edwards, p. 199.

16. Edwards, p. 201.

17. Greenfield, pp. 138–139.

18. Greenfield, p. 121.

19. *Computing Basics: PC Novice Learning Series* (Lincoln, NE: Sandhills, 1998), vol. 4, issue 3, p. 76.

20. *Computing Basics*, p. 81.

21. James Street, "Kids and Computers," *Parents' Perspective* radio program, September 10, 1997.

22. Rosenbaum.

23. Armstrong, p. 167.

24. Greenfield, p. 177.

25. Greenfield, p. 80.

26. Anderson, p. 46.

27. Anderson, p. 47.

28. Greenfield, p. 63.

29. Greenfield, pp. 42–43.

30. Armstrong, p. 178.

Chapter Eight

1. Thomas Armstrong, *Awakening Your Child's Natural Genius: Enhancing Curiosity, Creativity, and Learning Ability* (New York: Putnam's, 1991), p. xv.

2. Armstrong, p. xv.

3. John W. Gardner, *Excellence* (New York: Harper & Row, 1961), p. 170.

4. Elliot Eisner, "What Really Counts in Schools," *Educational Leadership* 48, no. 5 (February 1991): 17.

5. Judy Mann, "Finding a Place for Parents," *Washington Post*, May 21, 1993, p. E3.

6. Mann, p. E3.

7. James Earl Jones, actor, interview with authors, June 22, 1998.

8. J. Gardner, p. 59.

9. David Elkind, *The Hurried Child* (Reading, MA: Addison-Wesley, 1996), p. 55.

10. Rita Dunn, Kenneth Dunn, and Donald Treffinger, *Bringing Out the Giftedness in Your Child: Nurturing Every Child's Unique Strengths, Talents, and Potential* (New York: Wiley, 1992), p. 3.

11. Howard Gardner, cited in Cheri Fuller, *Unlocking Your Child's Learning Potential* (Colorado Springs: Navpress, 1994), p. 136.

12. J. Gardner, p. 51.

13. J. Gardner, p. 53.

14. Rhoda Kellogg and Scott O'Dell, *The Psychology of Children's Art* (New York: CRM–Random House, 1967), p. 87.

15. Joan Franklin Smutny, Kathleen Veenker, and Stephen Veenker, *Your Gifted Child: How to Recognize and Develop the Special Talents in Your Child from Birth to Age Seven* (New York: Ballantine, 1989), p. 99.

16. Armstrong, p. 99.

17. Cheri Fuller, *Unlocking Your Child's Learning Potential* (Colorado Springs: Navpress, 1994), p. 167.

18. Sheila Moore and Roon Frost, *The Little Boy Book* (New York: Ballantine, 1986), p. 142.

Chapter Nine

1. Sharon A. Edwards and Robert W. Maloy, *Kids Have All the Write Stuff: Inspiring Your Child to Put Pencil to Paper* (New York: Penguin, 1992), p. 17.

2. Kimberly Haeringer, "Beyond the School Building," *Washington Parent*, January–February 1997, p. 52.

3. Jaime Escalante, cited in C. M. Garcia-Prats and J. A. Garcia-Prats, *Good Families Don't Just Happen* (Holbrook, MA: Adams Media, 1997), p. 137.

4. Linda Dhion-Kenney, "Schools of Thought: Innovative Approaches to Learning," *Washington Post*, April 15 1991, p. B5.

5. John Holt, *How Children Learn* (New York: Dell, 1967), p. 91.

6. Holt, p. 23.

7. Holt, p. 140.

8. Thomas Armstrong, *Awakening Your Child's Natural Genius: Enhancing Curiosity, Creativity, and Learning Ability* (New York: Putnam's, 1991), p. 192.

9. Peter L. Benson, Judy Galbraith, and Pamela Espeland, *What Kids Need to Succeed* (Minneapolis: Free Spirit, 1994), pp. 138, 95, 143.

10. John W. Gardner, *Excellence* (New York: Harper & Row, 1961), p. 70.

11. J. Gardner, p. 70.

12. Rita Dunn, Kenneth Dunn, and Donald Treffinger, *Bringing Out the Giftedness in Your Child: Nurturing Every Child's Unique Strengths, Talents, and Potential* (New York: Wiley, 1992), p. vii.

13. Scott Willis, "The Well-Rounded Classroom: Applying the Theory of Multiple Intelligences," *Association for Supervision and Curriculum Development Update* 36, no. 8 (October 1994): 8.

14. J. Gardner, p. 61.

15. Armstrong, p. 184.

16. James M. Harris, *You and Your Child's Self-Esteem* (New York: Warner, 1989), p. 147.

17. Richard Carlson, *Celebrate Your Child: The Art of Happy Parenting* (San Rafael, CA: New World Library, 1992), p. 77.

18. Holt, p. 102.

19. Harris, p. 146.

20. Elliot Eisner, "What Really Counts in Schools," *Educational Leadership*, February 1991, p. 17.

Chapter Ten

1. Harris Clemes, Reynold Bean, and Aminah Clark, *How to Raise Teenagers' Self-Esteem* (Los Angeles: Price Stern Sloan, 1990), p. 33.

2. Fred Rogers and Barry Head, *Mister Rogers Talks with Parents* (Pittsburgh: Family Communications, 1983), p. 144.

3. Lawrence E. Shapiro, *How to Raise a Child with a High EQ: A Parents' Guide to Emotional Intelligence* (New York: Harper Perennial, 1998), p. 205.

4. Dorothy Corkille Briggs, *Your Child's Self-Esteem* (Garden City, NY: Doubleday, 1975), pp. 155, 164.

5. Amalya Nattiv, Gary F. Render, David Lemire, and Kristin E. Render, "Conflict Resolution and Interpersonal Skill Building through the Use of Cooperative Learning," *Journal of Humanistic Education and Development* 28, no. 2 (December 1989): 100.

6. Nancy Eisenberg, *The Caring Child* (Cambridge, MA: Harvard University Press, 1992), p. 127.

7. James M. Harris, *You and Your Child's Self-Esteem* (New York: Warner, 1989), p. 136.

8. Eisenberg, p. 54.

9. Ann F. Caron, *Strong Mothers, Strong Sons: Raising the Next Generation of Men* (New York: Harper Perennial, 1995), p. 193.

10. Caron, p. 188.

11. Briggs, p. 148.

12. Briggs, p. 140.

13. RaeLynn P. Rein and Rachel Rein, *How to Develop Your Child's Gifts and Talents during the Elementary Years* (Los Angeles: Lowell House, 1994), p. 38.

14. Kenny Luck, *52 Ways to Nurture Your Child's Natural Abilities* (Nashville: Nelson, 1994), p. 46.

Chapter Eleven

1. Richard Carlson, *Celebrate Your Child: The Art of Happy Parenting* (San Rafael, CA: New World Library, 1992), p. 2.

2. Sharon A. Edwards and Robert W. Maloy, *Kids Have All the Write Stuff: Inspiring Your Children to Put Pencil to Paper* (New York: Penguin, 1992), p. 17.

3. Fred Rogers and Barry Head, *Mister Rogers Talks with Parents* (Pittsburgh: Family Communications, 1983), p. 18.

4. Jack Youngblood and Marsha Youngblood, *Positive Involvement: How to Teach Your Children Habits for School Success* (Greenbelt, MD: Brown Wood, 1995), p. 23.

5. Youngblood, p. 21.

6. Joan Franklin Smutny, Kathleen Veenker, and Stephen Veenker, *Your Gifted Child: How to Recognize and Develop the Special Talents in Your Child from Birth to Age Seven* (New York: Ballantine, 1989), p. 51.

7. Wayne W. Dyer, *What Do You Really Want for Your Children?* (New York: Avon, 1985), p. 68.

8. Laura Sessions Stepp, "The Gift of Time," *Washington Post*, December 14, 1995, p. C5.

9. Trish Magee, *Raising a Happy, Confident, Successful Child: 52 Lessons to Help Parents Grow* (Holbrook, MA: Adams Media, 1998), p. 68.

10. Ann F. Caron, *Strong Mothers, Strong Sons: Raising the Next Generation of Men* (New York: Harper Perennial, 1995), p. 97.

11. David Elkind, *The Hurried Child* (Reading, MA: Addison-Wesley, 1996), p. 33.

12. Benjamin S. Bloom, *Developing Talent in Young People* (New York: Ballantine, 1985), p. 447.

13. Smutny, Veenker, and Veenker, p. 19.

14. Edwards, p. 21.

15. Edward, p. 19.

16. Lawrence E. Shapiro, *How to Raise a Child with a High EQ: A Parents' Guide to Emotional Intelligence* (New York: Harper Perennial, 1998), p. 162.

17. Steven A. Rosenberg and John M. Barry, *The Transformed Cell: Unlocking the Mysteries of Cancer* (New York: Putnam's, 1992), p. 33.

18. Magee, p. 63.

19. Arthur Kornhaber, *Between Parents and Grandparents* (New York: St. Martin's, 1986), p. 20.

20. Kornhaber, p. 27.

21. Kornhaber, p. 12.

22. Kornhaber, p. 50.

23. Sabatino Sofia, "Teacher Power," *Yale Alumni Magazine*, May 1998, p. 33.

24. T. Berry Brazelton, M.D., *Touchpoints: Your Child's Emotional and Behavioral Development* (New York: Addison-Wesley, 1992), p. 430.

25. Marian Wright Edelman, *The Measure of Our Success* (Boston: Beacon, 1992), p. 6.

26. Edelman, p. 6.

27. Shapiro, p. 38.

28. Shapiro, p. 44.

29. Shapiro, p. 38.

BIBLIOGRAPHY

Ahmad, Nyla. *Cybersurfer: The OWL Internet Guide for Kids.* Toronto: Owl Books, 1996.

Alvino, James, and the editors of *Gifted Children Monthly. Parents' Guide to Raising a Gifted Child.* New York: Ballantine, 1985.

Anderson, Joan, and Robin Wilkins. *Getting Unplugged: Take Control of Your Family's Television, Video Game, and Computer Habits.* New York: Wiley, 1998.

Apiki, Steve. "More Multimedia, Less Money: Familytested Hardware." *Family PC,* September 1996, pp. 141–144.

Armstrong, Thomas. *Awakening Your Child's Natural Genius: Enhancing Curiosity, Creativity, and Learning Ability.* New York: Putnam's, 1991.

Baldwin, Neil. *Edison: Inventing the Century.* New York: Hyperion, 1995.

Benson, Peter L., Judy Galbraith, and Pamela Espeland. *What Kids Need to Succeed: Proven, Practical Ways to Raise Good Kids.* Minneapolis: Free Spirit, 1994.

Berger, Debra R. "Ten Ways to Help Children Succeed in School." *Washington Parent,* September 1996, p. 17.

Bernstein, Leonard. *The Joy of Music.* New York: New American Library, 1967.

Bishop, Philip. "Build the Ultimate Software Library." *Family PC,* September 1996, pp. 97–112.

Bloom, Benjamin S. *Developing Talent in Young People.* New York: Ballantine, 1985.

Branch, Mark Alden. "Teacher Power." *Yale Alumni Magazine* (1998).

Brazelton, T. Berry. *Infants and Mothers.* New York: Dell, 1969.

Brazelton, T. Berry. *Toddlers and Parents: A Declaration of Independence.* New York: Dell, 1974.

Brazelton, T. Berry. *Touchpoints: Your Child's Emotional and Behavioral Development.* New York: Addison-Wesley, 1992.

Briggs, Dorothy Corkille. *Your Child's Self-Esteem.* Garden City, NY: Doubleday, 1975.

Burton, Jim. "Please, Mr. Postman." *Mac Home Journal* 4, no. 9 (September 1996): 68.

Campbell, James Reed. *Raising Your Child to Be Gifted.* Cambridge, MA: Brookline, 1995.

Carlson, Richard. *Celebrate Your Child: The Art of Happy Parenting.* San Rafael, CA: New World Library, 1992.

Caron, Ann F. *Strong Mothers, Strong Sons: Raising the Next Generation of Men.* New York: Harper Perennial, 1995.

Cassidy, Anne. "Solo Play." *Parents,* December 1993, pp. 99–102.

Chion-Kenney, Linda. "Schools of Thought: Innovative Approaches to Learning." *Washington Post,* April 1991, p. B5.

Clark, Faith, and Cecil Clark. *Hassle-Free Homework.* New York: Doubleday, 1989.

Clark, Gilbert A., and Enid D. Zimmerman. *Educating Artistically Talented Students.* Syracuse, NY: Syracuse University Press, 1984.

Clemes, Harris, Reynold Bean, and Aminah Clark. *How to Raise Teenagers' Self-Esteem.* Los Angeles: Price Stern Sloan, 1990.

Cline, Foster, and Jim Fay. *Parenting with Love and Logic.* Colorado Springs: Pinon, 1990.

Computing Basics: PC Novice Learning Series, vol. 4, issue 3. Lincoln, NE: Sandhills, 1998.

Dobson, Linda. *The Homeschooling Book of Answers*. Rocklin, CA: Prima, 1998.

Dreikurs, Rudolf, with Vicki Soltz. *Children: The Challenge*. New York: Hawthorn, 1964.

Dunn, Rita, Kenneth Dunn, and Donald Treffinger. *Bringing Out the Giftedness in Your Child: Nurturing Every Child's Unique Strengths, Talents, and Potential*. New York: Wiley, 1992.

Dyer, Wayne W. *What Do You Really Want for Your Children?* New York: Avon, 1985.

Earl, Felton, and Mary Carlson. "Towards Sustainable Development for American Families." *Daedalus* 122, no. 1 (Winter 1993): 107.

Eastman, P., and J. Barr. *Your Child Is Smarter Than You Think*. New York: Morrow, 1985.

Edelman, Marian Wright. *The Measure of Our Success*. Boston: Beacon, 1992.

Edwards, Sharon A., and Robert W. Maloy. *Kids Have All the Write Stuff: Inspiring Your Children to Put Pencil to Paper*. New York: Penguin, 1992.

Eisenberg, Nancy. *The Caring Child*. Cambridge, MA: Harvard University Press, 1992.

Eisner, Elliot. "What Really Counts in Schools." *Educational Leadership*, February 1991, pp. 11–17.

Elkind, David. *The Hurried Child*. Reading, MA: Addison-Wesley, 1996.

Erb, Karl. "Solitude." *Brandywine: Georgetown Day High School Literary Magazine* (Washington, D.C.).

Eyre, Linda, and Richard Eyre. *Teaching Children Joy.* New York: Ballantine, 1984.

Eyre, Linda, and Richard Eyre. *Teaching Children Responsibility.* New York: Ballantine, 1982.

Fox, Isabelle. *Being There.* New York: Barron's, 1996.

Fuller, Cheri. *Unlocking Your Child's Learning Potential.* Colorado Springs: Navpress, 1994.

Garcia-Prats, Joseph A., and Catherine Musco Garcia-Prats, with Clarice Cassidy. *Good Families Don't Just Happen.* Holbrook, MA: Adams Media, 1997.

Gardner, John W. *Excellence.* New York: Harper & Row, 1961.

Goldman, Linda. *Life and Loss: A Guide to Help Grieving Children.* Muncie, IN: Accelerated Development, Inc., 1994.

Gray, Donna B. *A Parent's Guide to Teaching Art.* White Hall, VA: Betterway, 1991.

Greenfield, Patricia Marks. *Mind and Media: The Effects of Television, Video Games, and Computers.* Cambridge, MA: Harvard University Press, 1984.

Griffith, Mary. *The Homeschooling Handbook.* Rocklin, CA: Prima, 1997.

Haeringer, Kimberly. "Beyond the School Building." *Washington Parent*, January–February 1997, p. 52.

Harrington, Maureen. "Families Driven to Keep Competitive in Sports." *USA Today*, April 27, 1998, p. 6D.

Harris, James M. *You and Your Child's Self-Esteem.* New York: Warner, 1989.

Healy, Jane M. *Your Child's Growing Mind.* New York: Doubleday, 1994.

Henri, Robert. *The Art Spirit.* Philadelphia: Lippincott, 1960.

Hill, Elizabeth Starr. *Evan's Corner.* New York: Viking, 1990.

Holt, John. *How Children Learn.* New York: Dell, 1967.

Kellogg, Rhoda, and Scott O'Dell. *The Psychology of Children's Art.* New York: CRM–Random House, 1967.

Kelly, Marguerite. *Marguerite Kelly's Family Almanac.* New York: Simon & Schuster, 1994.

Kornhaber, Arthur. *Between Parents and Grandparents.* New York: St. Martin's, 1986.

Krasnow, Iris. *Surrendering to Motherhood.* New York: Hyperion, 1997.

Lebrecht, Norman. *The Companion to 20th Century Music.* New York: DaCapo, 1996.

Leonard, Mary. "As More Children Are Overbooked, Play Gives Way to Achievement." *Boston Sunday Globe,* April 19, 1998, pp. G1–2.

Lord, Victoria. "Doing Well, Without TV." *Washington Post,* April 25, 1997, p. G5.

Luck, Kenny. *52 Ways to Nurture Your Child's Natural Abilities.* Nashville: Nelson, 1994.

Magee, Trish. *Raising a Happy, Confident, Successful Child: 52 Lessons to Help Parents Grow.* Holbrook, MA: Adams Media, 1998.

Mallis, Jackie. *Diamonds in the Dust: Discover and Develop Your Child's Gifts.* Austin, TX: Multi Media Arts, 1983.

Mann, Judy. "Finding a Place for Parents." *Washington Post,* May 21, 1993, p. E3.

Mead, Margaret. *Blackberry Winter: My Earlier Years.* New York: Simon & Schuster, 1972.

Moore, Sheila, and Roon Frost. *The Little Boy Book: A Guide to the First Eight Years.* New York: Ballantine, 1986.

Nattiv, Amalya, Gary F. Render, David Lemire, and Kristin E. Render. "Conflict Resolution and Interpersonal Skill Building through the Use of Cooperative Learning." *Journal of Humanistic Education and Development* 28, no. 2 (December 1989).

O'Brien, James F. *How to Design by Accident.* New York: Dover, 1968.

Oldenburg, Don. "Unleashing the Crayon Set." *Washington Post*, March 6, 1987, p. B5.

Palmer, Kimberly Shearer. "Perspective: A Father's Journal, A Guide to Living," *Washington Post*, April 17, 1998, p. B4.

Paulson, F. L., P. R. Paulson, and C. A. Meyer. "What Makes a Portfolio a Portfolio." *Educational Leadership* 48, no. 5 (February 1991): 60–63.

Peterson, Houston, ed. *Great Teachers.* New York: Vintage, 1946.

Piirto, Jane. *Understanding Those Who Create.* Dayton: Ohio Psychology Press, 1992.

Raskas, Bernard S. *Heart of Wisdom.* New York: Burning Bush, 1962.

Rein, RaeLynne P., and Rachel Rein. *How to Develop Your Child's Gifts and Talents during the Elementary Years.* Los Angeles: Lowell House, 1994.

Rogers, Fred, and Barry Head. *Mister Rogers Talks with Parents.* Pittsburgh: Family Communications, 1983.

Ronan, Colin. *The Atlas of Scientific Discovery.* London: Quill, 1983.

Rosenbaum, Karen. "Kids and Computers." *Parents' Perspective* radio program, September 10, 1997.

Rosenberg, Steven A., and John M. Barry. *The Transformed Cell: Unlocking the Mysteries of Cancer.* New York: Putnam's, 1992.

Rothstein, Edward. *Emblems of the Mind: The Inner Life of Music and Mathematics.* New York: Times Books, Random House, 1995.

Rowe, John W., and Robert L. Kahn. *Successful Aging.* New York: Pantheon, 1998.

Santo, Cristine. "Parental Guidance: Time to Start Typing?" *Family PC,* September 1996, pp. 167–168.

Shapiro, Lawrence E. *How to Raise a Child with a High EQ: A Parent's Guide to Emotional Intelligence.* New York: Harper Perennial, 1998.

Smutny, Joan Franklin, Kathleen Veenker, and Stephen Veenker. *Your Gifted Child: How to Recognize and Develop the Special Talents in Your Child from Birth to Age Seven.* New York: Ballantine, 1989.

Snelling, W. R. "Ideas and Perspectives: Strategies for the Next Six Years." *Independent School Management,* April 6, 1987, pp. 5–8.

Sofia, Sabatino. "Teacher Power." *Yale Alumni Magazine,* May 1998, p. 33.

Spock, Benjamin, and Steven J. Parker. *Dr. Spock's Baby and Child Care,* 7th ed. New York: Pocket Books, 1998.

"Sports and Fitness: Mobile, Agile, and Versatile." Program for the Parents Council of Washington, the Holton Arms School, Bethesda, MD, November 14, 1995.

Stepp, Laura Sessions. "The Gift of Time." *Washington Post,* December 14, 1995, p. C5.

Street, James. "Kids and Computers." *Parents' Perspective* radio program, September 10, 1997.

Takacs, Carol Addison. *Enjoy Your Gifted Child.* Syracuse, NY: Syracuse Press, 1986.

"The Heroes of the Revolution." *Family PC,* September 1996, p. 68.

Torrance, E. Paul. *Guiding Creative Talent.* Upper Saddle River, NJ: Prentice Hall, 1962.

Venditto, Gus. "Safe Computing." *Internet World,* September 1996, pp. 49–50.

Webb, Colin, and Wynne Rowe. *Computers & Kids: A Parent's Guide.* Australia: Angus & Robertson, 1995.

White, Burton L. *The First Three Years of Life.* Upper Saddle River, NJ: Prentice Hall, 1985.

Willis, Scott. "The Well Rounded Classroom: Applying the Theory of Multiple Intelligences." *Association for Supervision and Curriculum Development Update* 36, no. 8 (October 1994): 8.

Willoughby, Stephen S. "Family Math Awareness Activities." *National Council of Teachers of Mathematics.*

Youngblood, Jack, and Marsha Youngblood. *Positive Involvement: How to Teach Your Child Habits for School Success.* Greenbelt, MD: Brown Wood, 1995.

INDEX

ABOUT THE AUTHORS

Connie Reider Photography

The Burt family (L to R): Stephen, Andrew, Jonathan, Sandy, Jeff, and Daniel

With Stephen and Jonathan in New England, Daniel on the West Coast, and Sandy, Jeff, and Andrew in Washington, DC, the family enjoys treasured time together.

Steve Maclone Photography

The Perlis family (L to R): Cliff, Barry, Linda, Debbie, Roy, and Aaron

A daughter joins the family! Roy and Debbie have set up their home in Boston, Cliff and Aaron are attending school in Philadelphia, and Linda and Barry are in Maryland (missing them all!).

Sandy Burt and **Linda Perlis** produce and host *Parents' Perspective,* a weekly radio talk show on parenting issues. For a list of show topics and related information, visit their Web site at http://i.am/parentsperspective. To order a program cassette, send a $5.00 check or money order to: *Parents' Perspective,* P.O. Box 42257, Washington, DC 20015, or call (800) 791-8573.

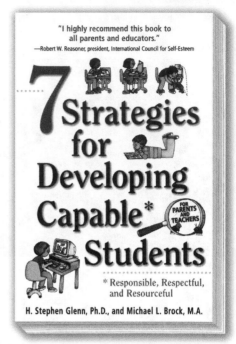